Armies of Early
Colonial North America
1607–1713

Armies of Early Colonial North America 1607–1713

History, Organization and Uniforms

By
Gabriele Esposito

Pen & Sword
MILITARY

First published in Great Britain in 2018 by
Pen & Sword Military
an imprint of
Pen & Sword Books Ltd
47 Church Street
Barnsley
South Yorkshire
S70 2AS

ISBN 978 1 52672 521 9

A CIP catalogue record for this book is
available from the British Library.

Printed and bound in India by Replika Press Pvt. Ltd.

Pen & Sword Books Limited incorporates the imprints of Atlas, Archaeology, Aviation,
Discovery, Family History, Fiction, History, Maritime, Military, Military Classics, Politics,
Select, Transport, True Crime, Air World, Frontline Publishing, Leo Cooper, Remember When,
Seaforth Publishing, The Praetorian Press, Wharncliffe Local History, Wharncliffe Transport,
Wharncliffe True Crime and White Owl.

For a complete list of Pen & Sword titles please contact
PEN & SWORD BOOKS LIMITED
47 Church Street, Barnsley, South Yorkshire, S70 2AS, England
E-mail: enquiries@pen-and-sword.co.uk
Website: www.pen-and-sword.co.uk

Contents

Gabriele Esposito is a military historian who works as a freelance author and researcher for some of the most important publishing houses in the military history sector. In particular, he is an expert specializing in uniformology: his interests and expertise range from the ancient civilizations to modern post-colonial conflicts. During recent years he has conducted and published several researches on the military history of the Latin American countries, with special attention on the War of the Triple Alliance and the War of the Pacific. He is among the leading experts on the military history of the Italian Wars of Unification and the Spanish Carlist Wars. His books and essays are published on a regular basis by Osprey Publishing, Winged Hussar Publishing and Partizan Press; he is also the author of numerous military history articles appearing in specialized magazines like *Ancient Warfare Magazine*, *Medieval Warfare Magazine*, *Classic Arms & Militaria Magazine*, *History of War*, *Guerres et Histoire*, *Focus Storia* and *Storie di guerre e guerrieri*.

Acknowledgements

This book is dedicated to my parents, Maria Rosaria and Benedetto, for their unconditioned love and support during all phases of my life. A very special mention goes to 'The Company of Military Historians' for giving me permission to use several colour plates from their magnificent collection devoted to the uniformology of the Americas. A special thank-you goes to Dave Sullivan, the administrator of 'The Company of Military Historians', who made all this possible with his generous efforts. A special thought goes to all the artists and experts who collaborated over the years to create this fantastic selection of plates; in particular, I want to express my personal admiration for René Chartrand, whose pioneering publications were of fundamental importance for the researches of this book.

Introduction

The main aim of this book is to study a very little-known period of North American military history: the early era of British and French colonization. Many people around the world think that the military history of the USA and Canada started with the French–Indian War or the US War of Independence: one of the objectives of this book is to show precisely how this general assumption is wrong, by illustrating in a concise but complete way all the main military events happening in North America during the years 1607–1713. I've decided, for reasons of space, to limit the analysis of this volume to the Thirteen Colonies and Canada, thus not including the Spanish colonies founded in the territory of the modern United States (like Florida): after all, their origins and development are quite similar to those of Spanish Central America and thus deserve another study entirely devoted to them.

Regarding the temporal arch of this book, it starts with the establishment of the first successful English colony in North America: Jamestown on 14 May 1607. After covering all the seventeenth century, our journey in colonial America will stop with the end of Queen Anne's War (1702–1713), which was nothing other than the North American theatre of operations of the Spanish Succession War. The Treaty of Utrecht, which ended that conflict, had very important consequences for North America, setting the stage for the future great wars of the eighteenth century that culminated in the French–Indian War and led to the start of the American Revolution in 1775.

In addition to the colonial American forces raised by the English and French, this book will also cover the regular units sent from England and France for service in the Americas. Obviously, this is not a book with the ambition of covering all military aspects related to the English and French armies of this period: the text will limit itself to the role that the European contingents had in the military development of the American colonies. In addition, some sections of this study will be devoted to two other European colonial powers which were 'minor' participants in the colonization of North America: Sweden and the Netherlands. For a long time the history of New Sweden and New Netherland has been considered a secondary episode in the formation of the USA and thus has never been studied in a complete way: this book will try to end this situation, at least regarding the military aspects of the colonization.

Finally, there will also be some space for the Indian tribes of North America: after all, most of the fighting which took place in the Americas during 1607–1713 was conducted against them. The Indians described in this book are very different from those who are present in our common imagery: in the seventeenth century, the real military power in the Americas was them, not the small European colonies that were just forming and developing. In fact, one of the greatest achievements of the early American colonial forces was that of resisting the superior military forces of the indigenous inhabitants. The great continental wars between European colonial powers happened only at a later stage, when the local enemies were no longer a serious menace for the existence of the European settlements.

'Columbus' expeditions to America 1492–1496', by H. Charles McBarron, *MUIA Pl. 281*, © The
Company of Military Historians.

Chapter 1

The early colonization of North America

The first explorations

The first European settlers in North America were the Vikings, who arrived on the eastern coast of Canada during their explorations of North Atlantic in the late tenth century. The Norse settlement in what was known as 'Vinland', however, ended with failure after only a few years of existence. In 1494, following Columbus's discovery of the New World two years before, the Treaty of Tordesillas was signed between the two major Catholic powers of Europe: Spain and Portugal. According to this treaty, which was ratified by the Pope, the kingdoms of Spain and Portugal divided the entire non-European world into two areas of exploration and colonization. The Spanish and Portuguese dominions were divided by a meridian along 370 leagues, known as 'raya': the lands to the east were to belong to Portugal, while those to the west were of the Spanish Crown. This division was very favourable for Spain in the Americas, because it gave only Brazil to the Portuguese. All the other European powers were thus excluded from the early colonization of the New World: but this was not to last for long. England and France, in particular, soon disputed the Spanish claims over the northern part of the continent, with the ambition of founding colonies on the Atlantic coast of North America.[1] Under letters patent from the French King Henry VII, the great explorer John Cabot became the first European known to have landed in Canada since the time of the Vikings. After 1497, Cabot and his son Sebastian continued to explore the waters and coasts of the North Atlantic. In the following decades, various explorers set sail from England and France for the New World, including Jacques Cartier, who in 1534 claimed the first North American territories for France.

The lost colony of Roanoke

The English colonization of North America received great impulse from Queen Elizabeth I, who financed exploring expeditions made by famous pirates/explorers of the time like Francis Drake. On 25 March 1584, the 'Virgin Queen' granted Sir Walter Raleigh a charter for the colonization of an area of North America which was to be called, in her honour, Virginia. Raleigh and Queen Elizabeth intended that the venture should provide riches from the New World, as well as new bases from which to send privateers on raids against the treasure fleets departing from the Spanish colonies in Central and South America. On 27 April

---

[1] Gallay, Allan, *Colonial Wars of North America 1512–1763: An Encyclopedia* (New York & London, 1996).

'Spanish troops in America 1597–1598', by H. Charles McBarron, *MUIA Pl. 73*, © The Company of Military Historians.

1584, Raleigh dispatched an expedition led by Philip Amadas and Arthur Barlowe to explore the eastern coast of North America. The explorers arrived at Roanoke Island on 4 July the same year, establishing relations with the local tribes of the Secotans and Croatoans. On 9 April the following year, a second expedition led by Sir Richard Grenville departed from Plymouth. After arriving on Roanoke Island, the English settlers initiated exploration of the mainland coast and native settlements; during these operations there was an incident with the Indians, which led to the burning of one of their villages. Despite the hostility of the Indian tribes and a general lack of food, Grenville decided to leave 107 men to establish a colony on Roanoke Island and returned to England, in order to embark more men and fresh supplies for the new colony.

In the following months, the colonists were attacked by the Indians in retaliation for the burning of one of their villages. Despite the enemy's superior numbers, the settlers were able to repulse the attacks of the Indians and maintain possession of their fort. Soon after the attack, Sir Francis Drake stopped at the colony while he was on his way home after a successful raid in the Caribbean. Drake offered to take the few colonists back to England, and several of them accepted. Grenville's relief expedition arrived shortly after Drake's departure, finding no settlers in the colony. It is highly probable that the few remaining ones were killed during a new assault by the natives. Grenville decided to return to England with the bulk of his forces, leaving behind just a small garrison to maintain an English presence on Roanoke Island. In 1587, Raleigh despatched a group of 115 settlers to establish a new English colony on Chesapeake Bay. These were led by John White and had orders to travel to Roanoke in order to check on the garrison left there by Grenville. After finding no surviving English soldiers, and fearing for their own lives, the majority of the colonists persuaded White to return to England: only 115 settlers were left behind at Roanoke. While White was in England the Anglo-Spanish War broke out, with the result that every able English ship had to join the fight against the Spanish Armada, leaving White without means to return to Roanoke. He was finally able to sail back to the Americas on 18 August 1590, but found the settlement again completely deserted. The only clue left by the 115 settlers was the word 'Croatoan' carved onto a stockade board. On the following day, White and his men abandoned the colony of Roanoke Island forever.

The Virginia Company

In 1606, King James I of England, understanding the importance of establishing a permanent settlement in North America, decided to grant competing royal charters to two different commercial companies: the Plymouth Company and the London Company. These were officially chartered on 10 April 1606 and were collectively known as 'The Virginia Company', their main function being to raise private funds from investors in order to settle Virginia. At that time the region known by this name comprised the entire eastern coast of the modern United States, from Spanish Florida in the south to the New France colonies in Canada. The two companies operated with identical charters but with different territories: the Plymouth Company was granted the territory located between the 38th and 45th

'Crews of Queen Elizabeth's ships in 1580', by Eric Manders, *MUIA Pl. 335*, © The Company of Military Historians.

parallels (roughly between the upper reaches of Chesapeake Bay and the current USA-Canada border), while the London Company received the lands between the 34th and 41st parallels (roughly between Cape Fear and Long Island Sound). An area of overlapping territory was thus created, which would then go to the first company that proved strong enough to colonize it.

The fortunes of the two companies proved to be quite different right from the beginning: the Plymouth Company, after establishing Popham colony along the Kennebec River on 13 August 1607, abandoned it more or less after only a year and became practically inactive for the rest of its history. The London Company, on the other hand, founded the famous Jamestown settlement on 14 May 1607: this was located about 40 miles inland along the James River, a major tributary of Chesapeake Bay in present-day Virginia. The terrain chosen to build the new colony was a defensible strategic point,[2] not inhabited by the nearby Virginian Indian tribes. At that time, the Indians of Virginia numbered more or less 14,000 and were politically organized into the powerful Powhatan Confederacy. The first settlers of Jamestown had serious difficulties during their early months in America: conflict with the Indians started almost immediately and, after a failed native attack against the settlement, continued as a guerrilla war of ambushes and conducted by small groups of Indian warriors.[3] Unable to hunt or farm in an effective way, the colonists soon found themselves with no food.[4] Luckily for them, Powhatton (the supreme chief of the Powhatan Confederacy) called a halt to guerrilla warfare operations, with the view of using the newcomers as allies in his wars against other Indian tribes.[5] Thanks to this change of attitude by the Indians, who started to trade with the settlers and gave them enough corn to survive, the Jamestown settlement had a better fate than the Roanoke colony. Despite this, loss of life had already been high: two-thirds of the settlers had died before the arrival of the first ships coming with supplies from England.

In September 1608, Captain John Smith became the new leader of Jamestown settlement. He was a professional soldier who had served as a mercenary in several European armies and thus had great experience of military matters. By the autumn of 1609, when the accidental explosion of a powder charge wounded Smith so badly that he had to return to England, Jamestown was strongly defended by fortifications and well garrisoned by trained militiamen.[6] Problems regarding food and other supplies, however, remained more or less the same. During the period 1609–1610, the Jamestown settlers faced rampant starvation: only sixty of the original 214 colonists survived. In June 1610, the remaining settlers decided to abandon Jamestown and set sail for England; while descending the James River, however, they met a relief fleet led by the new governor, Baron De La Warr, and thus went back to Jamestown with the new colonists and supplies.

---

[2] Roberts, Keith, 'The Virginia Militia', in *Military Illustrated*, Issue 61, 1993, p.21.
[3] Tisdale, D.A., *Soldiers of the Virginia Colony, 1607–1699* (Petersburg, 2000).
[4] Gallay, Allan, *Colonial Wars of North America 1512–1763: An Encyclopedia* (New York & London, 1996).
[5] Roberts, Keith, 'The Virginia Militia', in *Military Illustrated*, Issue 61, 1993, p.21.
[6] Ibid., p.24.

Map of Virginia made by John Smith (1612). Public domain picture obtained from Wikimedia Commons.

The Anglo-Powhatan Wars

De La Warr proved to be more belligerent toward the Indians than any of his predecessors, starting campaigns of conquest against them with brutal methods. Two neighbouring Indian villages and their cornfields were burned by small military parties sent from Jamestown, with the result that a full-scale war broke out between the Powhatan Confederacy and Jamestown settlement. In April 1613, after years of raids and ambushes, the English were able to capture Pocahontas, daughter of the Powhatan Confederacy's supreme chief. This caused an immediate suspension of hostilities, but peace negotiations stalled for months over the return of captured hostages and arms. In March 1614, an agreement was finally reached, sealed by the marriage of Pocahontas to the colonist John Rolfe. The First Anglo–Powhatan War had seen a rapid expansion of the territories controlled by the English settlers: in early 1609, Jamestown was the only area under British control, but by the end of the conflict, the Virginian Indians had lost much of their riverfront territories located along the James River.

Following the marriage of Pocahontas and Rolfe, peace and prosperity reigned for several years. After this period of positive coexistence, the new chief of the Powhatan Confederacy,

Opechanacanough, attempted to eliminate the English colony of Jamestown once and for all. On the morning of 22 March 1622, the Virginian Indians attacked and destroyed the outlying English plantations and communities up and down the James River, in what became known as the 'Indian Massacre of 1622'. Jamestown itself, however, was warned of the Indian attack and managed to avoid destruction. After his victory, Opechanacanough withdrew his warriors, sure that he had inferred a mortal blow to the settlers. Despite being shocked by the Indian attacks, however, the settlers soon began recovering and drew the population together into fewer settlements, for better defence against future attacks. The Indians continued hostilities with their usual guerrilla methods, but on a larger scale, which proved to be very effective. The colonists were prevented from growing the corn that they needed, with the result that hundreds of them died in the following months. In addition, diseases spread in the overcrowded new defensive settlements, which were nothing else than besieged forts.[7] The 'Massacre of 1622' brought unfavourable attention onto the Jamestown colony, particularly from King James I. Two years later, after a long debate, the king decided to dissolve the London Company and transformed Virginia into a royal colony. A new phase in the history of the North American colonies had begun.

The military organization of Jamestown settlement, 1607–1635

Since the beginnings of Jamestown settlement, it was clear to colonists that if they wanted to survive they had to organize themselves in some sort of military structure, in order to defend their new lands and with the objective of expanding them as soon as possible.[8] The first structure built by the settlers, which was completed on 15 June 1607, was a triangular fort with three bulwarks at each corner: four or five guns were mounted in them and all the colonists' houses were built inside the fort. According to John Smith, leader of the colony from 1608–1609, the Jamestown settlement was well armed, having more weapons than men available to use them: twenty-four cannons, 300 musket snaphances and firelocks, cuirasses, pikes, swords and morions (helmets).[9] Thanks to his great military experience, Smith was able to reorganize in an effective way the military structures of the new colony. The original fortifications were rebuilt as a pentagon and blockhouses were added as outworks to defend the passage joining the Jamestown peninsula to the mainland. Regular guard detachments were organized and all the able-bodied colonists were introduced to a military training programme. Smith taught the settlers how to handle their weapons in an effective way, as well as the first rudimentary tactics for fighting in wooded country. Since the Indians would have never fought in a battle on open terrain, Smith's solution to Indian ambushes was to strike at their villages and cause such damage that their leaders would sue for peace. Since the early months, the colonists at Jamestown adopted some military organization, including military

[7] Ibid., p.25.
[8] Tisdale, D.A., *Soldiers of the Virginia Colony, 1607–1699* (Petersburg, 2000).
[9] Chartrand, René, *Colonial American Troops 1610–1774 (1)* (Oxford, 2002), p.35.

'Virginia colonial militia 1611–1615', by H. Charles McBarron, *MUIA Pl. 109*, © The Company of Military Historians.

ranks such as captains, sergeants and corporals; however, it was the arrival of the new governor, De La Warr, which brought a rigid code of military discipline.

In 1610, this led to the drafting of the 'Lawes Divine, Morall and Martial', the earliest extant body of laws written in English in the western hemisphere. The Virginia laws were inspired by contemporary English military codes and were notable for their harshness. In any case, the first period of the new colony was characterized by many difficulties and this partly justified the severity of these early measures. According to the laws, the colonists were organized into six companies or 'bands' of fifty men, each under a captain. In addition, there was a small 'Guard of Halberdiers' escorting Governor De La Warr: what we know for sure is that the components of this unit were dressed in special red cloaks, bearing the livery of his Lordship the Baron.[10] A training programme was set up to ensure that all able-bodied colonists had to train and exercise regularly, with perfect military discipline. Each of the six companies in turn was on watch, fully armed and equipped, while the others performed the activities required for the subsisting of the settlement. The laws of 1610–1611 also spelt out the duties of each military rank and mentioned some of their relative arms and equipment, provided by the London Company. Officers had to be equipped like a 'targeteer': with helmet, light armour, quilted protective clothing and target (small round shield). In addition, they had to carry a snaphance or a firelock. Despite these regulations prescribing the use of armour, many officers chose to leave off some of it on campaign, in order to increase their mobility for the rapid kind of warfare conducted in early colonial America. They usually wore only some parts of the armour, most notably breast and back plates. Helmets, though, were always worn; judging by the surviving parts found by archaeologists, the most common models were burgonets for the officers and morions for the rankers.[11] The inclusion of a snaphance or firelock in the equipment of each officer probably meant that each one of them was also armed with a pistol (the snaphance or firelock were mounted only when use of the weapon was imminent, in order to avoid any kind of damage). As rank distinction, officers had gorgets and red sashes worn over the right shoulder. Sergeants had halberds for garrison duties but were armed like the officers when on campaign. The equipment of common soldiers was divided in two categories, corresponding to two different kinds of troops: musketeers and targeteers. Musketeers were equipped as follows: helmet, light armour of quilted protective clothing (including a canvas coatee), sword and musket. The main weapon was a heavy matchlock, which required the use of a rest to fire. Targeteers carried the following pieces of equipment: helmet, quilted protective clothing (especially for the legs), small round shield, sword and pistol or 'scuppet' (a short firearm having a folding stock). In general terms, the colonists preferred using quilted protections instead of the traditional European ones: armour was mainly worn as a protection against Indian arrows, and thus there was no need to wear heavy armour made of metal and designed for the European battlefields. In addition, warfare in colonial America consisted of raids and pursuits: a high level of mobility was required if the colonists wished to combat the Indians in an effective way.

---

[10] Ibid.
[11] Ibid., p.43.

The marriage between Rolfe and Pocahontas resulted in the establishment of what appeared to be a lasting peace with the natives, with the consequence that the military posture of the English colonists relaxed. By 1617 they had started to abandon the fortified settlements, concentrating themselves on growing tobacco for export. In 1619, Governor Yeardley formally dissolved the military organization created by De La Warr. The arms and accoutrements described in the laws of 1610–1611, however, remained more or less the same during the following two decades, being used in the First and Second Anglo-Powhatan Wars. Facing the emergency caused by the first of these two conflicts, the colonists required help from England and the shipment of new weapons: 2,000 helmets, 400 shirts of mail, forty suits of half-armour, 100 brigandines, 700 calivers, 300 pistols with firelocks, 300 heavy matchlocks, 400 bows and 1,000 bills were sent from England.[12] From this list we can denote several things, for example that helmets were used by practically every soldier of the colony. The shipment of 400 shirts of mail and 100 brigandines shows how light armour and protective clothing against arrows and spears were much required by the militiamen of Virginia. Brigandines and jacks were no longer considered as effective defensive equipment in England, but they were perfect for the militiamen fighting against the Indians in the Americas. As a result, many brigandines and jacks were provided by the Crown stores in England, on the basis that they were not suitable for use by the militiamen of the Trained Bands.[13]

The experiences of the two Anglo-Powhatan conflicts were decisive for the military development of Virginia: after 1622, it became clear that a new military organization was absolutely needed. All able-bodied colonists were militiamen, but also farmers whose absence would have severely damaged the productivity of their fields. The colonial authorities had to find a solution, which could reconcile the men's role as soldiers with their primary function of family men and farmers. As a result of these basic conditions, a new model of military structure was created, based on the practice of the English militia but with some local peculiarities.[14] In England, several householders could be grouped to provide a single soldier and his equipment; in Virginia, instead, all settlers had to be armed. As a result, the following solution was adopted: each colonist who went on service as a militiaman could rest assured that the other members of his community, who remained at home, would carry out the labours that were normally performed by him. In contrast to what happened in England, where militiamen stored their weapons in local armouries or the parish churches, in Virginia the militiamen kept their arms at home. This was due to the different kinds of threat that had to be faced: in England, the Trained Bands were assembled to face invasions from large foreign military forces, while the colonists in the Americas had to repel individual attacks from small groups of Indians. In 1629, a further refinement was added to this general organization, with the division of the colony of Virginia into four military districts, each under a local commander. Militia forces from the different districts could operate together for combined operations, as well as separately in response to local threats. In those same years, there was also a revival of

---

12   Ibid., p.35.
13   Roberts, p.25.
14   Ibid.

'Militia of Jamestown Colony 1607', by John Andrews, *MUIA Pl. 855*, © The Company of Military Historians.

interest regarding defensive fortifications: in 1631, the colonists began constructing a 6-mile line of fortifications which linked the James and York Rivers, with blockhouses set at regular intervals along it. With the building up of this new defensive line, the settlers secured a great part of the colony from the incursions of the natives.[15]

The Pilgrim Fathers

While all these events took place in Virginia, a group of Puritans known as the Pilgrims arrived in present-day Massachusetts on the ship *Mayflower* in November 1620, with the objective of establishing a new colony. The Pilgrims held Calvinist religious beliefs similar

[15] Tisdale, D.A., *Soldiers of the Virginia Colony, 1607–1699* (Petersburg, 2000).

to those of the Puritans, but, differently from them, were convinced that their religious congregation needed to be separated from the English state church. The Pilgrims were part of the Brownist English Dissenters, who had fled England due to the religious persecutions and emigrated to the much more tolerant Netherlands. Fearing to lose their English cultural identity with the progression of time, they decided to leave the Netherlands and go searching for a new land in the Americas.[16] As a result, they arranged with English investors to create a new settlement in North America, which was to be known as Plymouth colony. Robert Cushman and John Carver were sent to England to obtain a land patent, but their negotiations were delayed because of internal conflicts of the London Company. Finally, a patent was secured by the Pilgrims' representatives in June 1619. After a long period of preparation and difficult crossing of the Atlantic Ocean, the 102 Pilgrims embarked on the *Mayflower* finally sighted land on 9 November 1620. Some weeks later, on 21 December, the first landing party of the colonists arrived at the site of what later became the settlement of Plymouth. During the winter, the Pilgrims suffered greatly from lack of shelter, diseases such as scurvy and general lack of manpower. In February, after several encounters with the local Indians, the male residents of the new colony organized themselves into military orders. By the end of the month, the defensive position at Fort Hill had been completed, with the addition of five cannons landed from the *Mayflower*. On 16 March 1621, there was the first official encounter with the natives and the colonists learned that the supreme leader of the region was a Wampanoag chief named Massasoit. A meeting with the Indian chief was soon organized, thanks to the help of a native named Squanto, who had lived in England and thus knew how to speak English. The meeting had very positive results and a peace treaty was arranged between the colonists and Massasoit; according to it, each people would not bring harm to the other and Massasoit would send his allies to make peaceful negotiations with the settlers of Plymouth. During the first years of colonial life, fur trade was the dominant source of income: the colonists bought furs from the Indians and sold them on the European market. Farming and agriculture were not particularly developed, being at a subsistence level. The relationship with the Indians continued to improve, especially after a mission was sent to Massasoit's capital to establish stronger commercial ties. Massasoit agreed to an exclusive trading pact with the English colonists and promised to refuse any further contact with the French merchants, who were already becoming quite active in the region.

The military organization of Plymouth colony, 1620–1635

Since the foundation of the first settlement, the military leader of Plymouth colony was Myles Standish. He had training in military engineering from the University of Leiden and a good military knowledge. It was Standish who decided the defensive layout of the settlement soon after the *Mayflower* arrived at Plymouth. During the first winter in America, in February 1621, he organized all the able-bodied men into military orders. The 102 Pilgrim

---

[16] Gallay, Allan, *Colonial Wars of North America 1512–1763: An Encyclopedia* (New York & London, 1996).

The embarkation of the Pilgrim Fathers on the Mayflower. Public domain picture obtained from Wikimedia Commons.

Fathers who had landed at Plymouth were humble people used to a hard-working life and Spartan lifestyle. In everything they did, the Pilgrims never doubted that they were just carrying out the will of God. This resulted in an incredible determination, which enabled them to survive in the first difficult years of the settlement. In 1622, Standish organized the militia of Plymouth into four companies and helped to design the construction of a large palisade wall surrounding the settlement. To understand the kind of military life that was conducted in Plymouth colony, it is very useful to read the following passage written by Isaack de Rasiere in 1627:

> 'The men assemble by beat of the drum, each with his musket or firelock, in front of the captain's door; they have their cloaks on, and place themselves in order, three abreast, and are led by a sergeant without beat of drum. Behind him comes the governor in a long robe; beside him, on the right hand, comes the preacher with his robe on, and on the left hand the captain with his side-arms, and cloak on, and with a small cane in his hand; and so they march in good order, and each sets his arms down near him. Thus they are constantly on their guard night and day.'[17]

---

[17] Chartrand, René, *Colonial American Troops 1610–1774 (2)* (Oxford, 2002), p.3.

Portrait of Myles Standish. Public domain picture obtained from Wikimedia Commons.

As is clear from this description, military and religious life were strictly linked and the Pilgrims were tenacious men at arms. Like the militiamen in Jamestown, they used various types of firearms, edged weapons and armour. Helmets and corselets, in particular, remained in use until the mid-1630s. As time progressed, more 'trainband' companies like those of Plymouth were formed in the new villages that were built as the colony expanded in the surrounding areas.

Chapter 2

New France and the birth of Canada

The voyages of Jacques Cartier

After his first expedition in 1534, during which he had claimed the land around Gaspé Bay as property of the King of France, Jacques Cartier returned to Canada for a second voyage in 1535–1536. After reaching the St Lawrence, he sailed up-river for the first time and reached the Iroquoian capital of Stadacona. From mid-November 1535 to mid-April 1536, the French fleet laid frozen solid at the mouth of the St Charles River, under the Rock of Quebec. During this second expedition, the French built a fort and established good relationships with the Iroquoians. Impressed by the reports and descriptions of Cartier, King Francis I of France ordered the organization of a new expedition to Canada, with the objective of establishing a stable settlement. On 23 May 1541, Cartier departed for his third and last expedition to Canada. After arrival, he decided to settle on the site of present-day Cap-Rouge in Quebec. Some colonists and the convicts transported by his ships were landed to build a fortified settlement, which came to be known as Charlesbourg-Royal. In addition, a fort was built on the cliff overlooking the settlement for added protection. The Iroquoians were initially quite friendly towards the French, but gradually their attitude changed and the settlers started to suffer from a series of Indian attacks. As a result, Cartier became increasingly convinced that he had insufficient manpower to protect his settlement and go out for new explorations. He left for France in early June 1542, while the colony at Charlesbourg-Royal was abandoned the following year after disease, foul weather and hostile natives had made life impossible for the colonists.

Champlain and the foundation of Quebec

After Cartier's expeditions, French fishing fleets continued to sail to the North Atlantic coast and into the St Lawrence River, making alliances with the Indian Nations that they encountered. These early contacts were to become very important once France began to occupy the mainland in a stable way. French merchants soon realized that the St Lawrence region was full of valuable fur-bearing animals, especially the beaver, which were becoming rare in the European continent. By the 1580s, French trading companies had been set up and ships were contracted on a regular basis to bring back furs to France. In 1598, a trading post was established on Sable Island, off the coast of Acadia, but was unsuccessful. Two years later, a similar trading post was built at Tadoussac, but only five colonists survived after the first winter. In 1604, a settlement was founded on Saint Croix Island

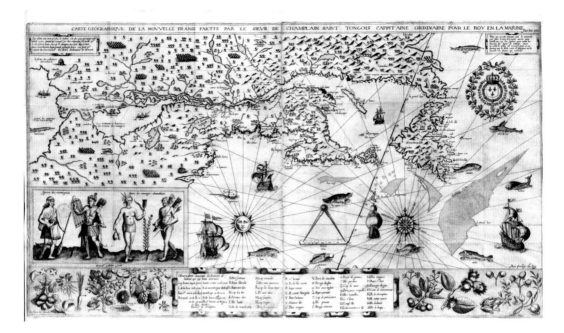

Map of New France made by Samuel de Champlain (1612). Public domain picture obtained from Wikimedia Commons.

(in present-day Maine), which was moved to Port-Royal (Acadia) in 1605 and finally abandoned in 1607.

After all these failed attempts to build a stable settlement, Samuel de Champlain, explorer and diplomat, founded the city of Quebec on 3 July 1608 with just twenty-eight men. Like the English colonies in Virginia, the early life of the Quebec settlers was extremely difficult: many of them died very early because of the harsh weather and diseases. This time, however, the French were able to resist and Quebec became their first stable colony in Canada. In 1610, the French led a second expedition to Port-Royal and re-established their colony there, which had been abandoned three years before. It was there, in 1613, that the first North American battle between English and French colonists was fought. Under orders from London, the English colonists of Jamestown launched a raid against the French positions in Acadia, including Port-Royal. The expedition was led by Samuel Argall, at that time 'Admiral of Virginia'. In October 1613, he surprised the French settlers at Port-Royal and sacked every building of the French colony. Despite the English victory, most of the French settlers managed to survive and the colony was not completely destroyed.

The first soldiers of New France

The first French exploring expeditions to Canada were not protected by regular troops, but by soldiers recruited by the trading and exploration companies that financed the various expeditions. The companies had to obtain permission from the king before recruiting

French arquebusier, mid–sixteenth century. Public domain picture from the Vinkhuijzen Collection of military uniforms, part of the New York Public Library digital collections.

English pikeman, early seventeenth century. Public domain picture from the Vinkhuijzen Collection of military uniforms, part of the New York Public Library digital collections.

military contingents and assumed all the costs of each expedition in exchange for an exclusive monopoly over some of the most lucrative commercial trades. For example, many of the companies which became active in Canada received a monopoly over the fur trade. In exchange for this privilege, the companies agreed to several obligations to the French royal house, including colonizing the new lands, Christianizing the Indians, and governing and defending the interests of the king. The leaders of these expeditions received royal commissions as lieutenant-generals or governors, exerting authority and acting in the name of the king.[1] As in the English settlements, rank and authority in the early colonies of New France were mostly military in nature. The first soldiers who served in Canada and who accompanied these expeditions were veterans of the French Royal Army who had already taken part in several military campaigns in Europe. In time of peace, the demobilized soldiers of the European armies were always looking for a chance to enlist, and overseas adventure was certainly appreciated by these experienced veterans.[2]

During his first voyage in 1534, Cartier took no professional soldiers with him; on the second expedition, however, he had a certain number of well-armed soldiers with pikes and halberds. Members of Cartier's third expedition included 300 men-at-arms, equipped with arquebuses, crossbows and small round shields. The new expedition had the objective of establishing a stable settlement, so a large amount of additional weapons was carried on the ships: 400 arquebuses, 200 crossbows, 200 small round shields and more than 1,000 pikes or halberds.[3] In addition, there were also several pieces of artillery. Regarding the clothing worn by Cartier's soldiers, we can state with a degree of certainty that they wore the first military uniforms ever used in Canada. Cartier gave to all the men-at-arms of his third voyage a black and white livery. At that time it was not uncommon for sailors and soldiers to wear the livery of the captain they were serving. Cartier chose black and white because they were the feudal colours of Brittany since the Middle Ages. He himself was from St Malo in Brittany, as were many of his soldiers; as a result, the livery of Brittany was a natural choice.[4] In the early decades of the seventeenth century, very few French soldiers were sent to Canada, for the simple reason that recruiting them was very expensive and the commercial companies were often on the verge of bankruptcy. This situation remained more or less the same until the death of New France's first governor, Samuel de Champlain, in 1635.

---

[1] Chartrand, René, *Canadian Military Heritage (Volume 1, 1000–1754)* (Montreal, 1993), p.48.
[2] Ibid., p.33.
[3] Ibid., p.35.
[4] Ibid.

Chapter 3

The growth of the New England colonies

The Great Migration of the Puritans

After Charles I became King of England in 1625, the religious conflict involving the Puritans worsened and Parliament started to increasingly oppose royal authority. With the religious and political climates so hostile and threatening, many Puritans decided to leave the country and go to North America. The success of Plymouth colony encouraged them to send more expeditions and settlers to the New World in order to form new communities where their faith could be practised in a free way. This phenomenon was known as the 'Great Migration' and lasted for two decades. As early as 1623, the Plymouth Council for New England (successor to the Plymouth Company) had established a small fishing village at Cape Ann under supervision of the new Dorchester Company. The latter had been organized thanks to the efforts of the Puritan minister John White of Dorchester, who, because of his acts in favour of the Puritans, has been called 'the father of Massachusetts Colony'. The Cape Ann settlement, however, soon proved unprofitable and the financial backers of the Dorchester Company terminated their support for the project by the end of 1625. Some of the settlers from Cape Ann decided to remain in the Americas and thus established a new colony a little further south, near the Indian village of Naumkeag, under guidance of Roger Conant. After this initial failure, White continued to seek funding for a colony: as a result, the Council for New England issued a land grant to a new group of investors that included a few holdovers from the Dorchester Company. The land grant was for territory between the Charles and Merrimack Rivers and the new company to which it was assigned was called The New England Company for a Plantation in Massachusetts Bay.[1]

In 1628, the new company sent 100 settlers to join Conant at Naumkeag settlement, which name was changed to Salem the following year. The Massachusetts Bay colony became the first English chartered colony having governors who did not reside in England: this independence helped the Puritan colonists to perform their religious practices with very little influence from the king and the Anglican Church. It is not clear if King Charles I knew that the company was intended to support Puritan emigration: he probably simply assumed that it was formed for business purposes only, as was the custom of the time. In 1630, after consolidation of the new colony at Salem, a flotilla of ships known as the 'Winthrop Fleet' sailed from England with more than 700 Puritan colonists. The fleet arrived at Salem in June 1630, starting the most important phase of the Puritan migration to the Americas. In the following

---

[1]   Gallay, Allan, *Colonial Wars of North America 1512–1763: An Encyclopedia* (New York & London, 1996).

ten years there was a steady exodus of Puritans from England, with about 10,000 people emigrating to Massachusetts and the new neighbouring colonies (which were often formed as a result of religious divisions arising among the colonists). The advent of the English Civil War in the early 1640s brought a halt to Puritan migration, with a significant number of men returning to England to fight in the conflict. The colonial authorities of Massachusetts were generally sympathetic to the Parliamentary cause and maintained positive relationships with the English Commonwealth and the Protectorate of Oliver Cromwell. In the years which followed, the economy of the colonies began to diversify and flourish, as the fur trading, lumber and fishing industries found important markets in Europe and the West Indies. The growth of a generation of people who were born in the colonies and the rise of a new wealthy merchant class began to slowly transform the political and cultural landscape of the New England colonies, whose governance continued to be dominated by relatively conservative Puritan leaders.

The new colonies

In the decades following the definitive establishment of Massachusetts Bay colony, various groups of settlers departed from Massachusetts in order to find new lands and create new settlements. This process gradually led to the formation of new colonies, which continued to expand for most of their history.

New Hampshire: The first settlements established in the area dated back to 1623, being mostly inhabited by fishermen who lived around the Piscataqua River; in addition, some plantations protected by small forts were built in the early 1630s. Since the beginning, the colonists of New Hampshire had to face serious military threats from the Indians and the pirates who were active in the region. In 1631, a professional soldier was sent to the new settlements in order to organize the militia and train the colonists of New Hampshire. In the following year, the New Hampshire Militia was already able to provide forty well-armed men for taking part in the chase of the pirate Dixie Bull (together with twenty militiamen sent from Boston).[2] Apparently, the colonists of New Hampshire were equipped very well. An inventory dating back to 1635 reveals that they had the following weapons and equipment: three sakers, three minions, two falconets, two rabinets, four mortars, twenty-two arquebuses, four muskets, sixty-seven carbines, six pairs of pistols, sixty-one swords, fifteen halberds, thirty-one helmets and eighty-two beaver bill spears.[3] In 1641, the settlements of the Piscataqua River area passed under the jurisdiction of Massachusetts and their men became part of the Massachusetts Militia. New Hampshire colony became again independent only in 1679, when it was separated from Massachusetts by royal order. As a result, on 16 March 1680, the independent militia of New Hampshire was re-formed: this initially consisted of one foot company for each of the four major settlements (Portsmouth, Dover, Exeter and

---

2   Chartrand, René, *Colonial American Troops 1610–1774 (2)* (Oxford, 2002), p.14.
3   Ibid.

English arquebusier, late sixteenth century. Public domain picture from the Vinkhuijzen Collection of military uniforms, part of the New York Public Library digital collections.

Hampton), plus an artillery company and a troop of horse stationed in Portsmouth. The cavalry company, however, was disbanded a few years later. With the progressive growing of the colony, more militia companies were formed; in 1689, these were all grouped together in the so-called New Hampshire Regiment of Militia. During the period 1690–1713, the 750 militiamen of New Hampshire were particularly active in the struggle against Indian raids, with some parties of them constantly scouting on the frontier. North of New Hampshire there was the area of Maine, which then formed part of Massachusetts Bay colony. This was very exposed to Indian attacks, especially since hostilities with the French colonists led to

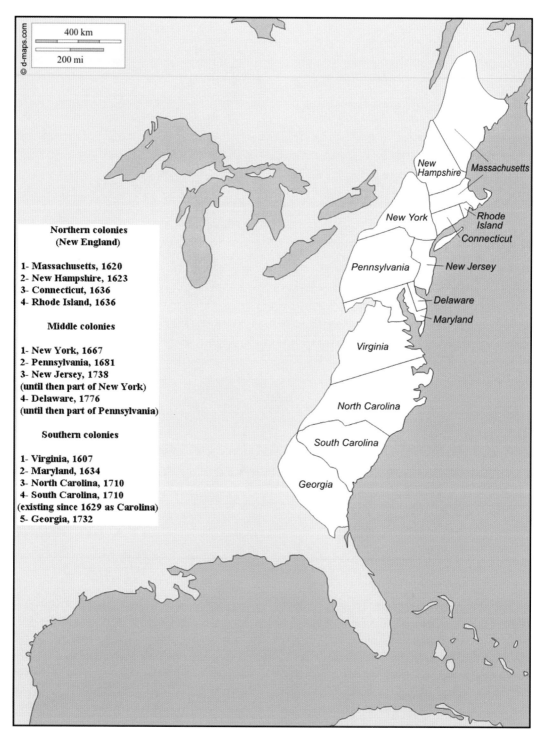

Northern colonies
(New England)

1- Massachusetts, 1620
2- New Hampshire, 1623
3- Connecticut, 1636
4- Rhode Island, 1636

Middle colonies

1- New York, 1667
2- Pennsylvania, 1681
3- New Jersey, 1738
(until then part of New York)
4- Delaware, 1776
(until then part of Pennsylvania)

Southern colonies

1- Virginia, 1607
2- Maryland, 1634
3- North Carolina, 1710
4- South Carolina, 1710
(existing since 1629 as Carolina)
5- Georgia, 1732

Map of the Thirteen Colonies, showing their internal subdivision and date of creation. Map modified by Gabriele Esposito; original obtained from http://d-maps.com/carte.php?num_car=30646&lang=en.

the beginning of continuous raid warfare on the northern borders of New England. Around 1671, the militia of Maine was composed of 700 men, divided as usual into companies: these were not separate units but part of Massachusetts' militia system.

Connecticut: Around 250 colonists, led by Thomas Hooker and coming from Massachusetts, settled on the west bank of the Connecticut River in early 1636. One of the reasons why Hooker had left Massachusetts Bay colony was that only members of the Puritan Church could vote and participate in the government of the colony; he believed, instead, that any adult male owning property should have had the right to vote and take part in the political life of the colony. No militia was initially formed by the Connecticut colonists, but relations with the local Pequot Indians became increasingly difficult. As a result, the settlers were soon ordered to assemble for training once a month. In April 1637, the Pequots attacked the settlements in Connecticut, obliging the colonists to raise a force of ninety militiamen for a month of service. John Mason, a veteran soldier who had fought in the Netherlands, was given command of this small militia force. On 23 May, the Pequots' main fortified town was assaulted and taken by the Connecticut militiamen led by Mason. Most of the Pequots (including children and women) were killed, and the great victory of the colonists transformed into a massacre for the Indians. Apparently, the ninety militiamen who destroyed the Pequots were all well equipped with armour, swords and muskets. Following the significant experience of the Pequot War, the assembly of the colony decreed that every militiaman on service should carry a sword and musket with its relative ammunition.

Once the Indian menace had largely disappeared, militia training in Connecticut became quite lax for several years. This situation changed from the mid–1650s onwards, when England's wars with the Netherlands led to tensions with neighbouring New Netherland. At that time the Connecticut Militia numbered more or less 800 men, including a troop of horse raised in Hartford during 1658. However, despite military preparations, there were no major clashes with the Dutch forces. In 1644, Connecticut colony had absorbed the smaller Saybrook colony, which had been formed in 1635 by John Winthorp the Younger, son of the Governor of Massachusetts Bay colony. Saybrook colony was small but located at the mouth of the Connecticut River, in a strategic position. In 1665, Connecticut colony also incorporated the independent territory of New Haven colony. The latter had been formed by Puritan settlers in 1638; four years later, its militia was already structured on four company-like 'squadrons'.[4] Each militiaman of the colony was responsible for his personal equipment, but the colony's government provided a pike to each individual. Pikes remained a common weapon in New Haven as late as 1663, by which time a certain number of artillerymen and mounted militiamen had also been added to the local military forces. In 1665, the militia of New Haven colony was incorporated into that of Connecticut. Following the Dutch recapture of New York in 1673, Connecticut's colonial authorities ordered that 500 militiamen (more or less a third of the colony's militia) had to be mounted to patrol the coast. During King Philip's War (see Chapter 7), in November 1675, Connecticut contributed to

---

4   Ibid., p.19.

the war efforts of New England by sending a force of 315 militiamen. In addition, around 350 militia 'dragoons' were employed against the Indians; these men had to provide horses, weapons, equipment and clothes for themselves, but could be compensated in case of loss of their properties.[5] During King William's War (see Chapter 13) and Queen Anne's War (see Chapter 14), Connecticut militiamen were frequently embodied, usually by draft, and served in other colonies. In 1690, around 200 militiamen were sent to Albany; in 1693, around 150 Connecticut 'dragoons' were also sent there. During the central years of Queen Anne's War, 800 militiamen patrolled the frontier of the colony (on horseback during summer, on snowshoes during winter).

Rhode Island: In January 1636, Salem minister Roger Williams was banished from Massachusetts because of his theological differences with the ruling class of the colony. He preached that government and religion should have been separated, and believed that the Wampanoag and Narragansett Indians had been treated by the English settlers with no justice. After being exiled from Massachusetts, the Narragansett Indians helped him to survive during winter and sold him some land for establishing a new colony in present-day Providence, Rhode Island. Williams and his group of colonists settled at the tip of Narragansett Bay and the new site was called 'Providence Plantation'. It soon became a place of religious freedom, but internal divisions among the colonists led to the formation of two new independent settlements: Portsmouth and Newport. In 1644, however, Providence, Portsmouth and Newport united for their common independence as the 'Colony of Rhode Island and Providence Plantations'. Since the early days of the Providence settlement, the colonists gave much importance to their military organization. In March 1638, the assembly of the colony ordered that every militiaman should have been provided with a musket and sword, plus the relative equipment and ammunition.[6] The militia of Rhode Island, differently from that of the other colonies, had few opportunities to gain military experience. Since the foundation of the colony, the relationship with the Narragansett Indians was quite positive because Roger Williams was able to keep them on friendly terms with his settlers. In 1637, the Indians formed a military alliance with the English and carried out an attack against the enemy Pequots, which nearly extinguished them. Some volunteer units of cavalry and artillery were later added to the militia of Rhode Island, including the Island Troop of Horse formed in 1667 at Newport and disbanded some years later.

Maryland: The colony of Maryland was founded in 1634 by a group of English Catholic refugees, under a charter obtained by Lord Baltimore from King Charles I. Officially, the colony is said to have been named in honour of Queen Henrietta Maria, the wife of Charles I. Each of the new colonists who settled in 1634 was very well equipped with musket, sword, bandolier with a powder flask and ammunitions.[7] By 1638, the St Mary colony had its own trained band

---

[5] Ibid., p.20.
[6] Ibid., p.22.
[7] Ibid., p.24.

'Somerset County Dragoons from Maryland Militia 1695–1697', by H. Charles McBarron, *MUIA Pl. 35*, © The Company of Military Historians.

of militiamen numbering 120 men. In the following years, the militia was expanded and thus received a better organization: in the early 1640s, captains were appointed for 'every hundred' men. In April 1650, the Maryland legislative assembly ordered the establishment of a small full-time garrison of six men under a captain, in the strategic fort at St Inigo Harbour.[8] As for Rhode Island, the Indians were not a serious military menace for the colonists of Maryland: the local natives had sold the land to the settlers and had simply moved away. In March 1655, the colony saw the beginning of a strong internal clash between Puritan and Catholic settlers, which ended with the victory of the former at the Battle on the Severn River. After the end of the hostilities, the militia was ordered to disarm any inhabitant suspected of disaffection towards the colony's Puritan government. As a result, Catholics, Quakers and Baptists were disarmed and their rights of citizenship denied until the American Revolution.

On 12 July 1658, the independent militia companies of Maryland were assembled together into two regiments, respectively known as the 'Northern' and the 'Southern'. In addition, there was also an independent 'governor's own company', which was not part of either regiment. All able-bodied men aged from 16–60 were to have weapons and hold monthly musters. It was established that drums and colours of both regiments were to be bought by using fines on defaulters. In 1661, the first detailed militia law was approved; five years later, the colonial authorities of Maryland purchased 140 snaphance muskets, 140 cutlasses, fifty cavalry carbines and a large quantity of ammunition.[9] All these weapons and equipment were stored as a reserve for the militia. Arms continued to be bought during the following decades, being paid for by a tax on tobacco exports. With the progressive expansion of the colony, new county regiments of militia were organized, which also included troops of cavalry and dragoons in addition to the usual foot companies. Cavalry troops were generally quite well equipped: at least one of them was fully equipped with weapons and accoutrements specifically imported from England. From 1692, a certain number of rangers (in practice mounted infantry) were posted to some forts built on the frontier.

---

[8]   Ibid., p.33.
[9]   Ibid.

Chapter 4

The Pequot War, 1636–1638

In the early 1630s, the Connecticut River Valley was in turmoil because the Pequots were aggressively expanding their area of control at the expense of neighbouring tribes: the Wampanoags to the north, the Narragansetts to the east, the Connecticut River Valley Algonquians and Mohegans to the west and the Algonquians of Long Island to the south.[1] All these tribes contended for political dominance and control over fur trading with the Europeans. During the previous two decades, a series of smallpox epidemics had severely reduced the total numbers of the Indians, due to their complete lack of immunity to the new disease. The English colonists, from Massachusetts Bay, Plymouth, Connecticut and the small Saybrook colonies, were gradually extending their control over the fur trade, with the ambition of expanding the territories of their colonies. Massachusetts Bay colony had obtained complete control over the trade of wampum (Indian beads worn as decoration and used as currency), which the Narragansetts and Pequots had controlled up until 1633. As a result, a series of incidents and small attacks increased tensions on both sides. John Stone, an English rogue, smuggler and privateer, was murdered with seven of his crew by the Niantic Indians, a western tributary group of the Pequots. The initial reactions in Massachusetts Bay colony varied from indifference to outright joy for Stone's death; in any case, the colonial officials decided to protest. The Pequots answered that the killing of Stone had been the result of a mistake, because they had attacked him thinking that he and his men were Dutch and not English.[2] The Pequots sent some wampum to atone for the killing, but refused the colonial authorities' demand that the warriors responsible for Stone's death be turned over to them for trial and punishment. On 20 July 1636, a respected trader named John Oldham was attacked while on a trading voyage to Block Island. He and several of his crew were killed and his ship looted by allies of the Narragansetts, who sought with this action to discourage English settlers from trading with their Pequot rivals. In the weeks that followed, colonial officers from Massachusetts Bay colony, Rhode Island and Connecticut assumed that the Narragansetts were the likely authors of the attack.

In August, Henry Vane, Governor of Massachusetts Bay colony, sent a party of ninety militiamen led by John Endecott to exact revenge on the Indians of Block Island. Endecott's men landed and attacked two Niantic villages: most of the Indians escaped, but the militiamen burned the villages to the ground. After the raid, Endecott went on to Fort Saybrook. The local colonists were not happy about the attack against the villages, but agreed that some of them would accompany Endecott's expedition as guides. The militiamen sailed along the

1   Pieroni, Piero, *I grandi capi Indiani* (Florence, 1963), p.29.
2   Ibid.

Skirmish against the Indians during the Pequot War. Public domain picture obtained from Wikimedia Commons.

coast to a Pequot village, where they repeated the demand of the previous year for those warriors responsible for Stone's death. Now they also demanded the ones responsible for the more recent killing of Oldham. After some discussion, Endecott concluded that the Pequots were stalling and decided to attack the village. As in the previous raid, most of the Indians escaped into the woods while the Massachusetts militiamen burned the village and crops. After this action, Endecott's men returned home. In the aftermath, the settlers of Connecticut colony had to deal with the anger of the Pequots. The latter attempted to get all the allied tribes to join their cause, but were only partially effective in their attempts.[3] The Western Niantic joined them, while the Eastern Niantic remained neutral. The traditional enemies of the Pequots, the Mohegan and Narragansetts, openly sided with the English colonists. The Narragansetts had lost significant territories to the Pequots in 1622 and were thus easily convinced by their friend Roger Williams to side with the English and fight on a large scale against the Pequots.

The Mystic massacre

During autumn and winter of 1636–1637, Saybrook colony was practically under siege: people who ventured outside the fort were killed by the Pequots. With the arrival of spring, the Indians increased their number of raids and started to attack the colonists of Connecticut.

---

[3]   Ibid., p.30.

In May, the leaders of the Connecticut River towns met in Hartford and decided to organize a force of militiamen to counter the Indian attacks. Captain John Mason was put in command of this force, which comprised ninety militiamen and seventy Mohegan Indians. At Fort Saybrook, the militiamen were joined by John Underhill with another twenty men. The expedition sailed to Narragansett Bay, where it gained further support from 200 Narragansett warriors. The force, now numbering 380 men, marched for approximately 20 miles towards

English arquebusier, early seventeenth century. Public domain picture from the Vinkhuijzen Collection of military uniforms, part of the New York Public Library digital collections.

Mystic Fort, with the intention of mounting a surprise attack against the Pequots just before dawn. The events which happened during the following day, 26 May 1637, became later known as the 'Mystic massacre'. The militiamen and their Indian allies surrounded one of the two fortified Pequot villages at Mystic; twenty Englishmen breached one of the gates in the village's palisade, but were repulsed by the Pequots. In order to cover their retreat, the militiamen used fire to create chaos and slow down the pursuit of the Indians. The ensuing conflagration trapped the majority of the Pequots inside the village and caused their death. Those few Indians who managed to escape were killed by the militiamen and their native allies who surrounded the village.[4] While the exhausted attackers were retreating to their boats, they were attacked by the Pequot warriors coming from the other fortified village. During these fragmented assaults, however, the Indians suffered very heavy losses against the relatively few suffered by the colonists. The Narragansett and Mohegan warriors with Mason and Underhill's colonial militia were horrified by the actions and way of fighting of the Englishmen, because according to them the foreigners were too furious and killed too many enemies.[5] The Narragansetts attempted to leave the militia column, but were attacked on their way home by pursuing Pequots. Underhill's men were then obliged to rescue their native allies: after being saved, the Narragansetts rejoined the colonists in their retreat and were used by them to carry the wounded, in order to free up more militiamen to repulse the attacks of the pursuing Pequots.

After such a serious defeat, the Pequots lost any motivation to fight and decided to abandon their villages to seek refuge in the territory of the Mohawks. In mid-June, 160 militiamen and forty Mohawk warriors departed from Saybrook with the objective of intercepting the Pequot refugees on their way to the Mohawk territory. The colonists caught up with the Pequots at Saska, capturing or killing the majority of them during the famous 'Fairfield Swamp Fight'. The Pequot chief Sassacus, however, was able to escape with eighty of his warriors and continued his march to the west. Sassacus reached the Mohawk territory, but there he was betrayed: the Mohawks killed him and sent his head to Hartford.[6] This practically ended the Pequot War, which resulted in the almost complete extinction of the proud Pequot tribe. After the Pequot War, there were no more significant conflicts between the Indians and the colonies of New England for about forty years. This long period of peace only came to an end in 1675 with King Philip's War.

---

[4]   Ibid., p.31.
[5]   Ibid.
[6]   Ibid.

Chapter 5

New Netherland

In the seventeenth century, the Netherlands lived an intense period of social, cultural and economic growth, known as the 'Dutch Golden Age'. The Republic of the Seven United Provinces had become a home to many intellectuals, international businessmen and religious refugees from other European countries. In 1609, English sea captain and explorer Henri Hudson was hired by the Dutch East India Company (in Dutch, *Vereenigde Oost-Indische Compagnie*, or VOC) to find a north-east passage to Asia. Hudson ended up exploring the waters off the east coast of North America. Upon returning to the Netherlands, Hudson reported that he had found a fertile land, inhabited by an amicable people ready to establish commercial relationships with the European traders. This stimulated interest in exploiting these new trade resources, acting as the catalyst for Dutch merchant-traders to fund more expeditions. In four voyages made between 1611 and 1614, the area between present-day Maryland and Massachusetts was explored, surveyed and charted by Dutch ships. The immediate and intense competition between Dutch trading companies, most notably in New York Bay and along the Hudson River, led to disputes and calls for regulation in Amsterdam. On 17 March 1614, the States General, the governing body of the Republic of the Seven United Provinces, proclaimed that it would grant an exclusive patent for trade between the 40th and 45th parallels. The patent was won by the New Netherland Company, which soon ordered a survey of the Delaware Valley.

Early settlement

Soon thereafter, Dutch traders built Fort Nassau on Castle Island, in the area of present-day Albany. The fort was built to defend river traffic against interlopers and to conduct fur trading operations with the natives. However, its location soon proved to be impractical. Similarly to the French in Canada, the main interest of the early Dutch colonists focused upon the fur trade: for this reason, they cultivated from the beginning good relations with the Five Nations of the Iroquois, in order to obtain access to the key regions from which the skins came. As early as 1615, the Dutch established a trading post on Manhattan Island; two years later, in 1617, they founded a second Fort Nassau on the east bank of the Delaware, near modern Philadelphia. However, the new site of the fort also proved to be impractical due to flooding and it was finally abandoned in 1618, in coincidence with the expiration of the patent given to the New Netherland Company. On 3 June 1621, the Republic of the Seven United Provinces gave a new patent to the Chartered West India Company, including the exclusive right to operate in the Americas. Unlike the English, the Dutch government preferred the formula of trading posts with

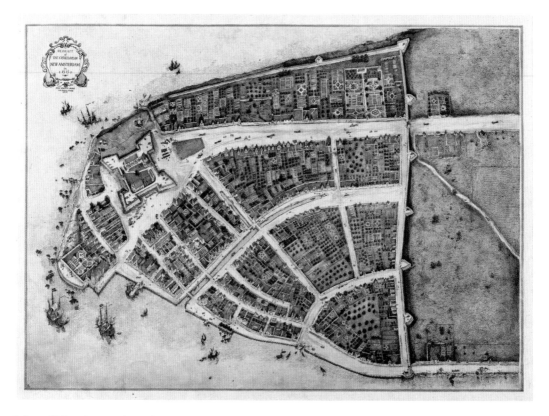

Map of New Amsterdam (1660). Public domain picture obtained from Wikimedia Commons.

small populations rather than encouraging mass immigration and establishing of large colonies. In 1624, the Dutch undertook settlement in a serious way, sending thirty families of Walloons to the Americas: some of them settled at Albany, thereafter known as Fort Orange; some at Fort Nassau, on the Delaware; some at Hartford; and the rest on Long Island and Manhattan Island. In 1626, Peter Minuit became Director of New Netherland and made a decision that greatly affected the development of the colony: he chose Manhattan Island, at the mouth of the Hudson River, as the location where the capital of New Netherland was to be built. Minuit purchased Manhattan Island from the Indians for trinkets worth about 24 dollars and founded New Amsterdam. He ordered the construction of Fort Amsterdam at the southern tip of the island, while the port city of New Amsterdam started to grow outside the walls of the fort. In the following years, departing from this centre, the Dutch traders and colonists organized flourishing commercial settlements in all directions. New Amsterdam soon became a major hub for trade between North America, the Caribbean and Europe. It was the place where raw materials were loaded, such as pelts, lumber and tobacco. This great commercial and economic growth of New Amsterdam was also helped by profitable privateering operations, sanctioned by the colonial authorities.

Dutch naval officer, mid-sixteenth century. Public domain picture from the Vinkhuijzen Collection of military uniforms, part of the New York Public Library digital collections.

The *Patroon* system and Kieft's War

With the objective of encouraging immigration, the Dutch West India Company established the 'Charter of the Freedoms and Exemptions' in 1629, which gave it the power to offer vast land grants and the title of '*patroon*' to some of its most important members. The title was associated to strong rights and privileges, including the possibility to create civil or criminal courts and to appoint local officers. In return, a Dutch *patroon* was required to establish a set-tlement of at least fifty families, whose members would have lived as tenant farmers. The new charter of 1629 also authorized the members of the company to purchase new lands from the Indians, with the aim of planting new colonies on them. The *Patroon* system, however, had negative effects on the life of the Dutch settlements from the beginning: the *patroons* started to dictate to the company, while jealousy and dissention became rampant among them. The new governors were sent out with vague instructions or with none at all, excepting that of making larger returns to their employers. Very frequently, the Dutch governors were men of selfish ambitions, tactless and incapable.

In 1638, Willem Kieft became Director of New Netherland. In the years preceding his appointment, the colony had continued to grow but was not particularly flourishing. For this reason, Kieft was under strong pressure from the Netherlands to cut costs. His first plan to do so was to demand tribute payments from the native tribes living in New Netherland. At that time a large number of tribes had signed mutual defence treaties with the Dutch and were thus gathering near the colony, a move also instigated by the widespread warfare that was going on among the tribes of the north.[1] Despite being warned by long-time colonists, Kieft pursued his objectives, which were rejected outright by the local Indian chiefs, who simply ignored his requests. Determined to force their submission, Kieft seized on the pretext of some pigs stolen from a farm to organize a punitive raid against a Raritan village on Staten Island, during which several Indians were killed. In August 1641, Claes Swits, a Swiss colonist who was very popular in New Netherland, was killed by Indians (probably as payment for an old 'blood debt'). As the colonists resisted his plans for war against the natives, Kieft tried to use the killing of Swits to build popular support in favour of his planned conflict against the Indians. The colonists had lived in peace with the Indians for nearly two decades, becoming business partners of the various tribes and sometimes even friends with Indian chiefs. In addition, the natives were far more numerous than the Dutch and could easily take reprisals against them and their property. The position of the colonists was represented by the 'Council of Twelve Men', the first popularly elected body of New Netherland. Unable to win the support of the Council, Kieft dissolved it and issued a decree forbidding its members to meet or assemble.

On 23 February 1643, two weeks after dismissing the Council, Kieft launched an attack on some camps of Indian refugees, Weckquaesgeek and Tappan natives who had been driven south during the previous year by the expansion of the Mohicans and Mohawks in the north. In what later became known as the 'Pavonia Massacre', the Dutch descended on the refugees' camps and killed 120 natives (including women and children). The operation had terrible

---

[1]   Ibid., p.35.

Dutch pikeman, first half of the seventeenth century. Public domain picture from the Vinkhuijzen Collection of military uniforms, part of the New York Public Library digital collections.

consequences for New Netherland: all the Algonquian tribes united themselves against the Dutch colonists, to an extent never seen before.[2] In the autumn of 1643, a force of 1,500 natives invaded New Netherland, killing many Dutch settlers and destroying everything they encountered, from entire villages to isolated farms. In just a few days, the work of two decades of settlement was eradicated. As New Amsterdam became crowded with refugees, the colonists decided to resist Kieft's rule in a more active way: they refused to pay the new taxes that he ordered and many of them began to leave the colony by ship.

---

2   Ibid.

Pound Ridge massacre

As a response to the crisis, Kieft recruited the Englishman John Underhill, a renowned military commander who had a key role in the Pequot War of 1637. Underhill departed the town of Stamford in New Haven Colony and arrived in New Netherland with orders to take command of the Dutch forces. He recruited militiamen on Long Island and later went with 120 men to the town of Greenwich. After much searching, the colonial force was finally directed to a party of Indians by some local residents. Underhill's men managed to kill or capture twenty Indians in a surprise attack. After this skirmish, the colonists launched a raid against the Weckquaesgeek and managed to destroy two villages, together with much of the Indians' stored food for winter. Following these events, in March 1644, Underhill led 130 men against an Indian village of the Wappinger Confederacy, located in the present-day town of Pound Ridge. The Dutch report of the operation states that the Indians had gathered in great numbers in that village, due to an ongoing special festival.[3] The night attack of the colonists was conducted under the light of a full moon, but the Indians were already awake when the colonial force launched its assault: in the initial phase of the battle, 180 natives were killed outside their houses. The colonists lost just one man and had only twelve wounded. The village was sufficiently surrounded by the European attacking force that it was impossible for the Indians to escape: those who survived the first assault holed up in their houses and fired arrows at the attackers. In a repetition of the tactics employed for the Mystic massacre, Underhill ordered the village set on fire with all its inhabitants inside. The Indians initially attempted to flee from the flames, but when they understood that there was no way out they decided to stay in the houses until overcome by the conflagration.[4] The enormous devastation wrought on the Indians at Pound Ridge compelled several chiefs to seek peace with the Dutch. Four Indian leaders arrived in Stamford and concluded a truce on 6 April 1644. The war would continue for another year, with neither side taking decisive action, until a final peace agreement was reached on 31 August 1645. Meanwhile, in the early months of the year, Kieft had already been replaced as the Director of New Netherland; however, he remained in office until the arrival of his successor in 1647. In many aspects, Kieft's War marked the beginning of the Dutch decline in North America: the colonial population had been greatly reduced and all the frontier settlements had been destroyed.

The Esopus Wars

During the years 1659–1663, the Dutch settlers were involved in two new Indian conflicts, this time against a tribe of the Lenape Indians. The wars were known as the Esopus Wars, from the name of the tribe fighting against New Netherland. The first Esopus conflict was a short-lived war between Dutch farmers and Indians, largely caused by the fear and misunderstanding of the settlers. Until 1659, relationships between the Dutch and the Esopus had

---

[3]   Ibid., p.36.
[4]   Ibid.

been quite positive; in that year, however, there was an incident which soon caused great tension. On 20 September, several Esopus men were hired to do some farm work for the Dutch colonists. After the Indians had completed their work, they received their pay in brandy: as a result, a drunken native fired a musket in celebration.[5] Despite the fact that no one was hurt, some of the Dutch settlers suspected foul play. A group of Dutch soldiers was sent to investigate among the Indians, but found no aggressive intentions. The farmers were not satisfied with this, and decided to attack the group of natives for no real reason.[6] Most of the Esopus escaped, but this event was just the beginning. The next day the Indians came back in great numbers, ready to start a war. Hundreds of Esopus warriors attacked, destroying crops, killing livestock and burning Dutch buildings. Outnumbered, the Dutch had little hope to stop the massive Indian attacks. However, they were able to resist and launch some small raids against the Esopus' fields, burning them in order to cause a shortage of food in the Indian villages. The First Esopus War ended on 15 July 1660, when the natives finally agreed to trade some disputed lands in exchange for peace and food. This peace was by no means definitive: many questions remained unsettled, resulting in the outbreak of a second but less important Esopus War.

The fall of New Netherland

As early as 1637, English colonists from Massachusetts Bay colony began to settle on lands claimed by New Netherland: sometimes they had permission from their own colonial government, but frequently they had no official authorization. Developing simultaneously with the Dutch ones, the English colonies grew more rapidly than New Netherland. As time progressed, the Dutch became increasingly concerned about an English invasion, especially after the formation of the New England Confederation in 1643. The English colonies of Connecticut and New Haven were actually located on lands claimed by New Netherland, but unlike the English colonists the Dutch were unable to populate or militarily defend them. The colonial authorities in New Amsterdam could do little more than protest. In 1650, both the English and Dutch decided to settle some of the most important questions with the Treaty of Hartford, according to which the Dutch provisionally ceded the Connecticut River region to New England, drawing New Netherland's eastern border approximately 250km west of the Connecticut's mouth. The Dutch West India Company refused to recognize the treaty, but failed to reach any other agreement with the English colonies. As a result, the Treaty of Hartford set the *de facto* border for the next few years.

In March 1664, King Charles II of England decided to annex New Netherland: on 27 August of the same year, four English frigates led by Richard Nicolls sailed into New Amsterdam harbour and demanded complete surrender of New Netherland colony. A lack of adequate fortifications, ammunition and manpower made New Amsterdam practically defenceless: this situation was the result of the usual indifference from the West India

---

[5]   Ibid., p.41.
[6]   Ibid.

Dutch arquebusier, first half of the seventeenth century. Public domain picture from the Vinkhuijzen Collection of military uniforms, part of the New York Public Library digital collections.

Company to previous requests from the colonists, who asked for reinforcement of men and ships. Director Stuyvesant negotiated positively with the English for good terms of surrender. In the Articles of Transfer, he and his council secured the principle of religious tolerance under English rule for all the Dutch colonists. The Articles were largely observed in New Amsterdam and the Hudson River Valley, but were almost immediately violated by the English along the Delaware River, where pillaging, looting and arson were undertaken. Many Dutch settlers were sold into slavery in Virginia, and an entire Mennonite settlement was wiped out. The 1667 Treaty of Breda ended the Second Anglo-Dutch War, but the Dutch did not press their claims on New Netherland, which remained in the hands of the English. Six years later, England and the Netherlands were again at war; during the new Anglo-Dutch War, the Dutch recaptured New Netherland in August 1673 with a strong fleet of twenty-one ships, the largest seen in North America until that time. Anthony Colve was chosen as the new governor and New Amsterdam was renamed as 'New Orange' (reflecting the installation of William of Orange as new stadtholder of the Netherlands). At the end of the Third Anglo-Dutch War, however, the economy of the Netherlands suffered from a series of problems and the state was practically bankrupt. As a result, according to the 1674 Treaty of Westminster that ended the conflict, New Netherland was again ceded to the English, and this time for ever.

The military organization of New Netherland

In the early years of New Netherland colony, no military forces garrisoned the new Dutch settlement. It was only in 1633 that the West India Company sent about fifty regular soldiers to garrison the colony. In the following years, the number of regular Dutch soldiers stationed in New Netherland increased considerably, from only twenty-eight in 1650 to 170 in 1659 and 250 by 1660.[7] However, this garrison was considered too expensive, being reduced to 130 soldiers from 1662. The few regulars were scattered in the various forts of the colony; as a result of their few numbers, Kieft was obliged to recruit Underhill and his English mercenaries to counter the Indians in the war of 1643–1645. In 1644, to fight against the Indians, the Dutch West India Company required 150 additional regular soldiers, armed with muskets and equipped with shirts of mail. From 9 May 1640, a new militia law required that all inhabitants of New Amsterdam had to be armed and formed into a Burgher Guard. This was to be organized by trade guilds, and the guilds' leaders had to be its officers. It consisted of all adult males who could afford to pay the fee to become a burgher. Except for night watch duties, the Burgher Guard was not mobilized until 1650, when two active companies of forty men each were formed. The first was provided with dark blue uniforms, the other with orange ones (thus being known as Blue Company and Orange Company).[8] In their first mission, they were sent to protect Long Island from feared attacks by the privateers, but these never materialized. In 1655, they participated with the regulars in the Dutch conquest of New Sweden. In 1658, the Burgher Guard of New Amsterdam was reorganized into three companies, each having its own distinctive colour of uniform. Equipment included partizans (polearms) for officers, halberds for sergeants and muskets for common soldiers. The large Dutch fleet that recaptured New Amsterdam from the British in 1673 transported an elite force of 600 marines, a strong detachment of which remained as garrison in the city until it

---

7   Chartrand, René, *Colonial American Troops 1610–1774 (1)* (Oxford, 2002), p.41.
8   Ibid.

'Dutch Corps of Marines in New Amsterdam 1670–1673', by Frederick Chapman, *MUIA Pl. 353*, © The Company of Military Historians.

was again ceded to England. The soldiers and militiamen of New Netherland were armed quite similarly to the contemporary English colonial forces in North America, with match-lock or flintlock muskets. During the early years, buff coats and helmets were quite popular, but apparently were not enough to protect them from the arrows of the Indians. Additional mail shirts were requested from the Netherlands: 200 of these were sent in 1641 for the sol-diers, as well as for all the freemen who would have paid to have them. By 1656, however, mail protection was no longer in use[9].

---

[9]   Ibid., p.43.

Chapter 6

New Sweden

By the middle of the seventeenth century, the Kingdom of Sweden had reached its greatest territorial extent and was one of the major military powers of Europe. The Swedes sought to expand their influence by creating an agricultural and fur-trading colony in North America. For this reason, the Swedish West India Company was founded and received the mandate to establish colonies between Florida and Canada for the purposes of trade. In particular, the Swedes were interested in the area along the Delaware River. The first Swedish expedition to the Americas sailed from the port of Gothenburg in 1637. On 29 March 1638, the Swedish ships anchored at a rocky point on the Christina River (a tributary of the Delaware); the colonists soon built a fort on the site of present-day Wilmington, which they named Fort Christina in honour of their queen. The first governor of the newly established settlement was Peter Minuit. Having been Director of New Netherland, Minuit knew the status of the lands on either side of the Delaware River: he knew very well that the Dutch had established deeds for the lands east of the river (in modern New Jersey), but not for those to the west (in present-day Maryland, Delaware and Pennsylvania). Minuit established himself on the west bank of the Delaware River and gathered all the chiefs of the local Indian tribes. He persuaded them to sign deeds that he had already prepared, in order to buy new lands for Sweden and prevent any territorial issue with the Dutch. Kieft objected to the landing of the Swedes, but Minuit ignored him since he knew that the Dutch were militarily impotent. The Swedes completed Fort Christina in 1638, when Minuit went back to Sweden to organize a second expedition. Unfortunately for New Sweden, the capable governor died during his voyage.

The conflict with New Netherland and the fall of New Sweden

During the next seventeen years (1638–1655), twelve more Swedish expeditions left the homeland for North America. A total of eleven vessels transported around 600 Swedish and Finnish colonists, who settled in New Sweden and made it flourish. The Swedish colony consisted of farms and small settlements located along both banks of the Delaware River, and rose to its greatest extent during the governorship of Johan Printz (1643–1653). He expanded the colony northward from Fort Christina along both sides of the Delaware and improved the colony's military and commercial prospects. Printz ordered the building of Fort Elfsborg, near present-day Salem on the New Jersey side of the Delaware, in order to seal the river against English and Dutch ships. The main military threat to the colony came from the Dutch, because the Swedish colonists had very good relationships with the Indians. In April 1648, the Dutch built Fort Beversrede just opposite the Swedish Fort New Korsholm;

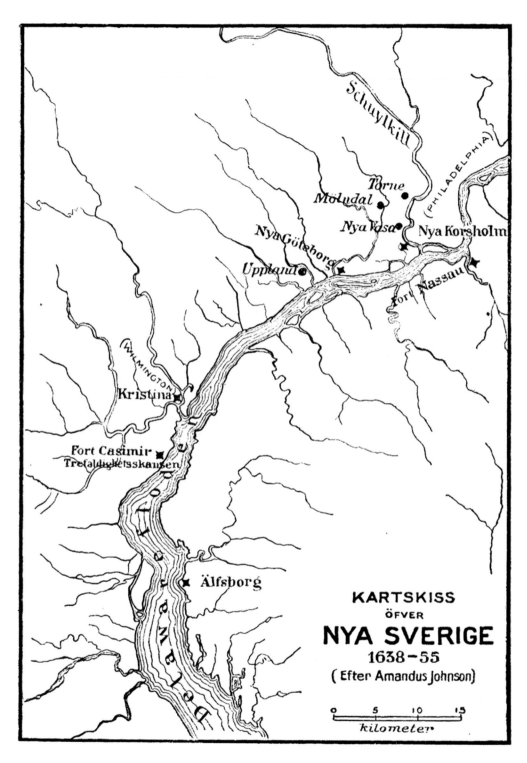

Map of New Sweden colony on the banks of the Delaware River. Public domain picture obtained from Wikimedia Commons.

'Swedish garrison at Fort Christina 1642–1643', by Eric Manders, *MUIA Pl. 513*, © The Company of Military Historians.

in May, the former was destroyed by the Swedes, who had considered it a provocation. The stubborn Dutch settlers rebuilt Fort Beversrede, but it was again razed by the Swedes in November of the same year. Despite these border tensions, open war between New Sweden and New Netherland did not break out. The Swedish settlement continued to flourish, but always had a very small population (numbering barely 200 souls in 1653). In 1654, Printz was succeeded by the colony's last governor, Johan Rising, at a time when the Dutch capital of New Amsterdam was ruled by the hot-tempered Peter Stuyvesant. Soon after arriving in New Sweden, Rising attempted to expand his colony by attacking the Dutch territories of New Netherland. The first step in this direction was the seizure of the Dutch Fort Casimir (present-day New Castle, Delaware), which had been built below Fort Christina on the western shore of the Delaware River. With no gunpowder, the Dutch garrison was obliged to surrender without firing a shot and Fort Casimir was occupied by the Swedes, who renamed it Fort Trinity. The furious Stuyvesant had his revenge during the summer of 1655, when he sent an expedition with seven armed ships and 317 soldiers on the Delaware River. The Dutch forces had orders to conquer the colony of New Sweden. Realizing that any kind of resistance would have proved useless, the vastly outnumbered Swedes surrendered Fort Trinity and, two weeks later, their main base of Fort Christina. New Sweden was henceforth absorbed into New Netherland, but the Swedish and Finnish presence in the territory remained. In fact, Stuyvesant permitted the Swedish settlers to continue as a 'Swedish nation' inside New Netherland and gave them permission to be governed by a court of their own choosing. The Swedish colonists were free to practice their religion, organize their own militia, retain their land holdings and continue trading with the native tribes. This autonomous 'Swedish nation' continued to exist until the English conquest of New Netherland in 1664.

The military organization of New Sweden

The military presence in New Sweden was always quite small, right from its formation: the first Swedish expedition of 1637–1638, for example, included just a small body of twenty-four soldiers. The colonial soldiers of New Sweden were armed and equipped as most other European troops of the time. In general terms, however, the Swedes in North America tended to have older weapons than the other European colonial contingents. They still had matchlock muskets in 1654, though there was the intention to convert them to flintlock during the following year.[1] With the exception of helmets, armour was kept to a minimum, and was usually for ceremonial wear only.[2]

---

[1] Ibid.
[2] Ibid.

Chapter 7

King Philip's War

Background

After the end of the English Civil War, the English settlers of Massachusetts Bay colony experienced a series of political problems. As we have seen, the Puritan colonists of Massachusetts supported with great determination both the English Commonwealth and the Protectorate of Cromwell; naturally, this presented problems upon the restoration to the throne of Charles II in 1660. The king sought to extend royal influence over the colonies, something that Massachusetts resisted more than the other colonies of New England. For example, the colonial government of Massachusetts repeatedly refused requests by Charles II and his agents to allow the Church of England to become established on Massachusetts territory.[1] In addition, New England colonists resisted adherence to any new law that could constrain colonial trade. For the Puritan colonists, the king had no authority to control the governance of the North American settlements. In 1643, the colonies of Massachusetts Bay, Plymouth, Connecticut and New Haven had formed a new military alliance known as the New England Confederation. Its main objective was to unite the Puritan colonists in support of their church and for defence against the Indians and Dutch. In addition, its charter provided for the return of fugitive criminals and indentured servants, serving as a forum for resolving inter-colonial disputes. Regarding relationships with the Indians, these had greatly changed over time. Initially, the Puritan colonists had tried to maintain peace with the natives, respecting them and their territories; however, as time progressed, the balance of power changed considerably. During the Great Migration, thousands of colonists had settled in New England, while the Native Americans had suffered severe population losses as a result of epidemics of smallpox, rubella, typhoid and measles. For almost half a century after the colonists' arrival, Massasoit of the Wampanoags had maintained an uneasy peace with the English settlers, in order to benefit from their trade goods and as a counter-weight to his tribe's traditional enemies: the Pequots, Narragansetts and Mohegans. To achieve this political objective, he had to accept colonial incursions into his territory and the growing political interference of the Englishmen. Massasoit died in 1661, being replaced as supreme chief of the Wampanoag Confederacy by his eldest son, Wamsutta. The latter, however, died the following year, opening the way to the ascendancy of his younger brother, Metacomet, later known as King Philip. Well known by the English authorities long before he became paramount chief of the Wampanoag Confederacy, Metacomet distrusted the colonists and began negotiating with the other Algonquian tribes against Plymouth colony. His political moves

---

[1]   Gallay, Allan, *Colonial Wars of North America 1512-1763: An Encyclopedia* (New York & London, 1996).

English sergeant, first half of the seventeenth century. Public domain picture from the Vinkhuijzen Collection of military uniforms, part of the New York Public Library digital collections.

were caused by the colonists' refusal to stop buying lands from the Indians and establishing new settlements. It soon became clear to Metacomet that the only way to arrest the English expansion was to start a great war of destruction, at the head of a large Indian military confederation comprising all the most important tribes.

The first phase of the war

John Sassamon, a so-called 'praying Indian' (a Native American convert to Christianity) serving as translator and adviser to Metacomet, reported to the Governor of Plymouth Colony that the Wampanoag chief was planning to gather allies for attacks on the widely dispersed colonial settlements. As a result, Metacomet was brought before a colonial public court to be judged: court officials admitted that they had not enough proof against the Indian chief, but warned him that if they had any further reports about military preparations they would confiscate Wampanoag lands and guns. Not long after the trial, Sassamon's body was found in the ice-covered Assawompset Pond. Plymouth colony officials arrested three Wampanoag Indians for his murder, including one of Metacomet's counsellors. On the testimony of a friendly Indian, a jury that included six Indian elders sentenced the three murderers to death: they were executed by hanging on 8 June 1675 at Plymouth. In response to the trial and executions, a band of Pokanoket Indians attacked several isolated homesteads in the small Plymouth colony settlement of Swansea on 20 June. After laying siege to the town for five days, they completely destroyed it and killed several inhabitants. On 27 June, a full eclipse of the moon occurred in the New England area: various tribes interpreted it as a good omen for attacking the English colonists, with the aim of destroying their settlements once and for all. Officials from the Plymouth and Massachusetts Bay colonies responded very quickly to the attack on Swansea: on 28 June, they sent a punitive military expedition that destroyed the important Wampanoag town of Mount Hope. As a consequence, the conflict soon spread, involving also the Podunk and Nipmuc tribes.

While the attack against Mount Hope was taking place, the colonists sent Ephraim Curtis to the west of Boston into Nipmuc territory, in order to negotiate a peace with that tribe and obtain assurances of loyalty to the English crown. When Curtis' party arrived, the Nipmuc village was already empty, but the colonists were still able to arrange a meeting with the Nipmuc chief Muttawmp. However, Curtis did not know that it was too late for any kind of negotiation: the Nipmuc warriors had already attacked an English settlement at Mendon and had decided to join Metacomet's rebellion. Curtis was later joined by Captain Thomas Wheeler and Captain Edward Hutchinson. On 14 July, Curtis and his men met with chief Muttawmp, who considered himself to be already at war with the English. The chief considered it better to feign friendship to the colonists and told them that he would show himself in Boston within seven days.[2] After Curtis' return to Boston, the colonial authorities were informed of the agreement that he had made with the Nipmuc chief. However, they decided that it was better not to wait for Muttawmp's arrival: Wheeler and Hutchinson were sent

---

[2]   Pieroni, Piero, *I grandi capi Indiani* (Florence, 1963), p.45.

with thirty mounted militiamen to negotiate directly with the Indian chief. Again, after discussing with the new English party, Muttawmp continued his deception but agreed to meet Hutchinson in Brookfield on the following day.

When the colonists arrived at the agreed place, they found no trace of Muttawmp or his men: at that point Hutchinson and Wheeler decided to march on the Nipmuc camp. In order to reach the camp, the English had to cross a swamp, taking a narrow path in single file. Despite protests from the Indian guides who were with the expedition,[3] the two English captains decided to take the risk. As a result, shortly after starting their march on the path, the militiamen were attacked by the Nipmuc warriors, who were very well armed with bows and muskets. When the Englishmen turned and tried to flee along the narrow path, they encountered another group of Nipmucs blocking their retreat. The ambush was very well planned and, apparently, the English colonists had no chance of escaping from the trap. They were so completely disorganized that they were not even capable of returning fire. In addition, both Hutchinson and Wheeler were seriously wounded. The entire force would have been destroyed, had it not been for the Indian guides who were with the militiamen, one of whom assumed command of the militia company and managed to lead the rest of it out of the trap and into the hills near the swamp.[4] The militiamen, including various wounded, retired to Brookfield, fully aware that Muttawmp and his warriors were in close pursuit. The village of Brookfield was relatively isolated, which meant that no help would be coming soon, even if the colonists of other New England towns could have got word of the attack.

Once at Brookfield, the militiamen tried to prepare some kind of defence and were joined by about seventy villagers who had learned of the coming Nipmuc attack. Wheeler retook command and tried to despatch two of his men to ask for help and reinforcements; however, they did not leave the village before the arrival of the assaulting Indians, and thus no request for help was sent from Brookfield. All the English defenders gathered in the house of John Ayers, one of the men who had been killed during the Indian ambush. When they arrived in the village, some of the Nipmucs kept the garrisoned house under constant fire, while the others drove off the livestock and looted the other houses of the settlement. After burning most of the village, Muttawmp gathered all his warriors and launched three assaults against Ayers' house. However, these were all repulsed by the English, who suffered just two casualties. On the second day of the siege, at dawn, Muttawmp had his men fill a wagon found in the village with combustible material, in order to direct it at the fortified house. However, the Indian plan did not work because of heavy rains which began while the wagon was being prepared.[5] During the ensuing confusion, Curtis managed to sneak out of the house and made a successful run for the woods. He went to Marlborough in order to ask for reinforcements, but by that time the colonial militia had already been alerted by some travellers who had heard gunfire near Brookfield. As a result, a group of militiamen led by Major Simon Willard was already on its way to relieve the Englishmen. The relief force arrived on the night of the third day, forcing the Indians to

---

[3] Ibid., p.46.

[4] Ibid.

[5] Ibid.

break off the siege. Further reinforcements continued to arrive in the following hours, including a certain number of Mohegan Indians who were allies of the colonists.[6] The fight between the militiamen (now numbering around 350 men) and the Indians continued until the middle of the night of the fourth day, but neither side was able to defeat or dislodge the other. At that point Muttawmp, who felt that his primary objectives had already been achieved (including obtaining crucial supplies from the looting of Brookfield), decided that there was no sense in risking the life of his remaining warriors and withdrew from the battlefield.

After withdrawing from Brookfield, Muttawmp led his party to Hatfield. Metacomet himself, with forty Wampanoag warriors, arrived there a short while later. Hearing of the attack, King Philip rewarded the Nipmuc chief and his men with unstrung wampum. In the following weeks the Indian offensive against the English settlements continued: throughout the rest of the year, the natives had a string of victories, mainly thanks to the skilful leadership of warrior chiefs like Metacomet and Muttawmp. They exploited to the full their knowledge of local terrain to achieve surprise and local superiority, often ambushing the colonial forces sent to track them down. The colonial authorities of New England had started to consider very seriously the situation: the colonies of Massachusetts Bay, Plymouth, New Haven and Connecticut all declared war on the Indians on 9 September 1675. The colony of Rhode Island, settled mostly by Puritan dissidents, tried to remain neutral but was dragged inexorably into the conflict. In early September, the colonists organized an expedition to recover crops from abandoned fields along the Connecticut River, which were of fundamental importance in view of a long war against the Indians. During a similar operation, on 12 September, the Battle of Bloody Brooke took place between eighty militiamen from Massachusetts Bay colony and a large group of Indians led by Muttawmp.[7] The colonists were escorting a train of wagons that carried the harvest from Deerfield to Hadley, in preparation for the subsequent winter of war. The Indians ambushed the militiamen and killed at least forty of them. The next Indian attack was launched on 5 October against the Connecticut River's largest settlement of the time: Springfield, Massachusetts. The Indians burned to the ground almost all of the city's buildings, but the majority of the inhabitants were able to escape. They took cover at the house of Miles Morgan, who had constructed one of Springfield's few fortified blockhouses. Similarly to what had happened in Brookfield, the colonists seemed trapped by the besieging Indians: however, one of Morgan's Indian servants was able to escape and alert the colonial troops of Massachusetts Bay colony. These, under command of Major Samuel Appleton, soon marched to Springfield and drove off the attackers.

The Great Swamp Fight

On 2 November 1675, Plymouth colony Governor Josiah Winslow led a combined force of over 1,000 colonial militiamen and about 150 Pequot and Mohegan Indians against the

[6] Ibid., p.47.
[7] Ibid., p.48.

English arquebusier, mid–seventeenth century. Public domain picture from the Vinkhuijzen Collection of military uniforms, part of the New York Public Library digital collections.

Narragansett settlements located around Narragansett Bay. The Narragansett tribe had not yet been directly involved in the great Indian conflict, but had allegedly sheltered many of King Philip's supporters and several Narragansett warriors had reportedly been seen during the Indian raids of the previous months.[8] The colonial authorities distrusted the Narragansett and were sure that the tribe would have joined King Philip's forces during the following spring. As a result, it was decided to pre–emptively strike the Narragansett before they could

---

[8]   Ibid., p.50.

attack the settlers and abandon their neutral status. The large militia force marched around Narragansett Bay, but the only thing that the militiamen were able to find was abandoned villages: the Narragansett had retreated to a large fortified settlement located in the centre of a swamp, near South Kingstown (modern Rhode Island). Led by a native guide known as 'Indian Peter', the militiamen were able to find the fortified village of the Narragansett on 19 December. This was the order of battle of the colonial forces:

Massachusetts Regiment, Major Samuel Appleton
- 1st Company, Major Samuel Appleton
- 2nd Company, Captain Samuel Mosely
- 3rd Company, Captain James Oliver
- 4th Company, Captain Isaac Johnson
- 5th Company, Captain Nathaniel Davenport
- 6th Company, Captain Joseph Gardner
- Cavalry troop, Captain Thomas Prentice

Plymouth Regiment, Major William Bradford Jr
- 1st Company, Captain Robert Barker
- 2nd Company, Captain John Gorham

Connecticut Regiment, Major Robert Treat
- 1st Company, Captain John Gallup
- 2nd Company, Captain Samuel Marshall
- 3rd Company, Captain Nathaniel Seely
- 4th Company, Captain Thomas Watts
- 5th Company, Captain John Mason
- Pequot Indian Company, Captain James Avery

On a bitterly cold storm-filled day, the Englishmen attacked the Indian village by surprise: the assault was made possible by the fact that an unusually cold late autumn had frozen the swamp, enabling the colonists to reach the defensive positions of the Narragansett.[9] After a fierce fight, the natives were finally overrun, with high casualties; the Indian settlement was burned and all its inhabitants were killed or evicted. In addition, most of the tribe's winter stores were destroyed. Some of the Narragansett warriors were able to escape with their families, but many of them died during the following days from wounds (combined with the harsh conditions of life in a frozen swamp). What became later known as the 'Great Swamp Fight' had reached its objective: for the rest of the conflict, the Narragansett tribe was forced out of its ambiguous position and had to join the English in the war against King Philip. Lacking supplies for an extended winter campaign, the colonial forces returned to their homes. Throughout the winter of 1675–1676, however, the Indians of Metacomet continued

---

[9] Ibid., p.51.

English pikeman, mid-seventeenth century. Public domain picture from the Vinkhuijzen Collection of military uniforms, part of the New York Public Library digital collections.

their raids and destroyed several frontier settlements in their continued effort to expel the English colonists from native lands.

The second phase of the war

In February 1676, Metacomet led a force of 1,500 Wampanoag, Nipmuc and Narragansett Indians in a dawn attack on the isolated frontier village of Lancaster in Massachusetts. The main fight took place around five fortified houses, including that of the local minister. This was set on fire and most of its occupants were slaughtered by the native warriors. Many of the village's other houses were destroyed in a similar way, before the Indians finally retreated northward. The spring of 1676 marked the high water mark for the Indian alliance when, on 12 March, the natives attacked Plymouth Plantation. Though the town withstood the assault, the Indians had demonstrated their ability to penetrate deeply into colonial territory.[10] In the following weeks the Indians attacked more settlements: Longmeadow, Marlborough and Simsbury. During similar operations, the Indians killed Captain Pierce and a company of Massachusetts militiamen between Pawtucket and the Blackstone's settlement. Several settlers were tortured and buried at Nine Men's Misery in Cumberland as part of the natives' ritual treatment of enemies. On 29 March, the Indians burned the abandoned city of Providence to the ground; at the same time, a small party of them infiltrated and burned part of Springfield while the militia was away. This was probably the most difficult moment for the New England colonies during the war: the few hundred colonists of Rhode Island, for example, became an island community for some time and were completely isolated. The Connecticut River towns, with their thousands of acres of cultivated crop land (the bread basket of New England), had to reorganize their agricultural production by limiting their crop lands and working in large armed groups for self-protection. Towns such as Springfield, Hatfield, Hadley and Northampton fortified themselves and reinforced their militias. Small settlements like Northfield and Deerfield were abandoned, with the surviving settlers retreating to larger towns.

Luckily for the colonists, some important native tribes supported their cause against King Philip. The New York Mohawks, traditional enemies of many of the warring tribes, proceeded to raid isolated groups of enemy Indians in Massachusetts, Rhode Island and Connecticut. The main military response of the colonists consisted of a series of raids conducted together with their native allies, which had devastating effects for King Philip's alliance. Traditional Indian crop-growing areas and fishing places in Massachusetts, Rhode Island and Connecticut were continually attacked by roving patrols of New England militiamen, combined with their native allies. When found, any Indian crops were destroyed: as a result, the tribes supporting Metacomet had few chances of finding any place to grow enough food or harvest sufficient migrating fish for the coming winter.[11] Many of the warring tribes thus drifted north into Maine, New Hampshire, Vermont and Canada. Other groups moved west into New York colony to avoid the attacks of the Iroquois, who had allied themselves with the English colonies.[12] On 21 April 1676, the Indians launched an attack on Sudbury in Massachusetts: the town was surprised by the raiders at dawn, but the military preparations of the previous months enabled the colonists to resist. Nearby towns sent reinforcements to help the defenders, but these relief forces were ambushed by the Indians surrounding the town. Captain Samuel Wadsworth, at the head of sixty militiamen, was killed with half of his men during one of these ambushes. Meanwhile, the Indians made their way through much

[10] Ibid., p.53.
[11] Ibid., p.54.
[12] Ibid.

of Sudbury, but were held off by the remaining defenders until the arrival of further rein-forcements. At the end of the battle, the native attackers were obliged to retreat after having inflicted serious losses on the colonists.

On 18 May, Captain William Turner and 150 volunteer militiamen from Massachusetts Bay colony attacked a large Indian fishing camp at Peskeopscut on the Connecticut River (modern Turner Falls in Massachusetts). In the ensuing battle, the militiamen killed around 100–200 Indians, as retaliation for earlier native attacks against Deerfield and other colonial settlements. However, Turner and nearly forty of his men were killed during an ambush while going back home. On 12 June, the colonists defeated an Indian attack at Hadley thanks to the help of the Mohegans; most of the survivors from the Indian attacking party were scattered into New Hampshire and further north. Later in the same month, a force of 250 Indian warriors was routed by the colonists near Marlborough. English successes contin-ued in the following weeks, and the new tactics employed by the colonists seemed to work perfectly. Combined forces of militiamen and Indian allies continued to attack, kill, capture or disperse the various bands that were supporting King Philip. These mainly included Narragansett, Nipmuc and Wampanoag natives. The Indians were usually attacked by the colonists while attempting to plant new crops or return to their traditional settlements.[13] The colonial authorities granted amnesty to each Indian individual surrendering to them, but those who had participated in raids or attacks against the colonial settlements were usually hanged or shipped off to slavery in Bermuda.[14] As a result of this new situation, King Philip's allies began to desert him. Over 400 Indians had already surrendered to the colonists by early July, and Metacomet was thus obliged to take refuge in the Assowamset Swamp below Providence. After learning this, the colonists organized more raiding parties of militiamen and Indian allies to storm the new enemy positions. The storming parties were allowed to keep the possessions captured from warring Indians and received a bounty on all captives.

Benjamin Church and the birth of the American rangers

The kind of warfare conducted by the Indians of King Philip obliged the colonists to change their tactics in a radical way, because the latter had proved to be too slow to counter the rapid assaults made by the natives, which destroyed many colonial settlements during the early phase of the war. For this reason, some of the most experienced colonial commanders started to form small parties of militiamen, very flexible and suitable for use against highly mobile groups of Indians.[15] One of the greatest innovators in this sense was Benjamin Church, con-sidered as the 'father' of the American rangers. During King Philip's War, he acted as the principal aide to Governor Josiah Winslow of Plymouth colony. Holding the rank of captain, he commanded a company of 200 militiamen (formed in July 1676) which was independent

---

[13] Ibid.
[14] Ibid., p.55.
[15] Zaboly, Gary, *American Colonial Ranger* (Oxford, 2004).

English pikeman, early seventeenth century. Public domain picture from the Vinkhuijzen Collection of military uniforms, part of the New York Public Library digital collections.

from the governor's direct command.[16] Church designed his force primarily to emulate Indian patterns of war: he endeavoured to learn fighting like Indians from Indians.

Under tutelage of their Indian teachers, Church's militiamen became the first ranger company in the military history of colonial America. This was a special full-time unit mixing white colonists selected for their frontier skills with friendly Indians; their main task was launching offensive strikes against hostile Indians in terrains where normal militia units proved to be

---

[16]   Chartrand, René, *Colonial American Troops 1610–1774 (3)* (Oxford, 2003), p.21.

English arquebusier, early seventeenth century. Public domain picture from the Vinkhuijzen Collection of military uniforms, part of the New York Public Library digital collections.

ineffective. Of the 200 men under Church's command, only sixty were English: the rest were allied Indians.[17] During the conflict, Church's men were the most successful in raiding the Indians' camps located in difficult terrains such as forests or swamps. Church was also the first colonial officer allowed to recruit Indians into the militia units, using them not only as explorers but also as fighters.[18] He persuaded many neutral or formerly hostile natives to join his company as irregulars; some of these even converted to Christianity. Thanks to their support, Church's rangers were able to track Indians into the forests and ambush them on various

---

[17] Ibid.
[18] Zaboly, Gary, *American Colonial Ranger* (Oxford, 2004).

Portrait of Benjamin Church in 1675. Public domain picture obtained from Wikimedia Commons.

occasions. The tactical success of the rangers reached its peak with the killing of Metacomet, which effectively brought the war in New England to an end. In fact, King Philip was killed at the end of an operation conducted by Church's elite company: on 12 August 1676, after being tracked down by the colonists, he was shot at Mount Hope by one of Church's Indians, named John Alderman.[19] The rangers had played a crucial role in the final victory of the New England colonies: as we will see, they were also later employed during King William's War and Queen Anne's War against the French and their Indian allies.[20] Church's men used their own clothing and weapons, having no uniforms: the only common items of equipment were mocassins and small hatchets, use of which was recommended by Church.

Enduring consequences

For a period of time, King Philip's War seriously damaged the prospects of most colonists in New England: hundreds of them had been killed and more than half of their villages had

---

[19] Chartrand, René, *Colonial American Troops 1610–1774 (3)* (Oxford, 2003), p.21.
[20] Zaboly, Gary, *American Colonial Ranger* (Oxford, 2004).

been completely destroyed. After 1676, the settlers incurred an enormous self-imposed tax burden to pay for the supplies that they had bought during the conflict; this held back the economy of the entire New England region for many years to come. However, thanks to their successful government and extraordinary population growth rate, the settlers were soon able to repair all the material damage. The human losses were replaced and the destroyed settlements rebuilt: in a few years the colonists restarted their process of expansion into the Indian territories. For the Indians, the defeat in King Philip's War was a mortal blow: the severe human losses suffered during the conflict wiped out entire tribes, as well as any hope of freeing North America from the foreigners. After the war, it became clear to all the Indian chiefs that the Englishmen were on their lands to stay and that there was no possibility of countering them with the use of violence. Most lands in Massachusetts, Connecticut and Rhode Island were now completely open to colonial expansion and settlement, something unthinkable just before the beginning of the war.[21]

The colonists' successful defence of New England, achieved with the use of their own resources, brought them to the attention of the royal government. Before King Philip's War, the North American colonies had been generally ignored, being usually considered as uninteresting and poor outposts. The situation changed completely after the end of the conflict, with a general increase of government control from England: the colonists, however, maintained direct control over local legislative and judicial bodies. Despite many efforts made in London, the government-sponsored Anglican Church remained of little importance in the Americas: Puritan congregational or dissident churches retained complete independence and supremacy in New England.

To sum up, the English colonists had demonstrated to the world that their settlements were becoming a real nation, with strong ties to the lands where they were located. They had won not only due to greater military power, but also their ability to outlast the natives in many aspects. The Indians typically had less than a year's worth of food supplies and no independent access to black powder, steel weapons or tools (for which they depended on trade with the colonists).[22] At the beginning of the war, the English settlers suffered many military defeats and lost hundreds of men, but despite no military help from England they were finally able to win, thanks to the general improvement of their military tactics and their system for provisions.

The military organization of Plymouth colony, 1635–1691

Since 1643, the militiamen of Plymouth colony started to be equipped with muskets and replaced their older firearms. In 1658, a troop of horse was added to the existing militia forces, as well as a senior staff headed by a major. During King Philip's War, Plymouth colony suffered very severe human losses: the basic organization of the militia remained more or less the same, but a new 'Company of Volunteers' numbering about 200 men was raised in July

---

[21] Pieroni, Piero, *I grandi capi Indiani* (Florence, 1963), p.58.
[22] Ibid., p.60.

English arquebusier, early seventeenth century. Public domain picture from the Vinkhuijzen Collection of military uniforms, part of the New York Public Library digital collections.

1676 for full-time service.[23] This was the famous ranger company created and led by Benjamin Church, which played a crucial role in the second part of the war against Metacomet and his allies. Of the 200 militiamen of this corps, no more than sixty were Englishmen, the rest being allied Indians from various tribes. Unlike the surrounding colonies, that of Plymouth remained quite small and thus saw no expansion of its military forces after King Philip's War. In 1691, it was finally absorbed into its most important neighbour, Massachusetts Bay colony.

The military organization of Massachusetts Bay colony, 1628–1713

The settlement of Massachusetts colony was relatively unopposed by the Indians in 1628; from the outset, however, all able-bodied men of the new colony bore arms. The first group of Puritan settlers arrived in America with the following weapons: eighty 'bastard snaphance'

---

[23]   Chartrand, René, *Colonial American Troops 1610–1774 (2)* (Oxford, 2002), p.3.

muskets (having 4ft barrels but no rests), ten matchlock muskets (having 4ft barrels and rests), sixty suits of pikeman's armour (varnished in black), sixty pikes, twenty half-pikes and some halberds or partizans (bought by the Massachusetts Bay Company).[24] In addition, all the militiamen of the early colony were also armed with swords: the majority of these were straight and slim-bladed thrusting weapons, but others were broad and heavy cutlasses for slashing cuts. For additional protection, many militiamen employed privately purchased helmets and buff leather coats. As the Massachusetts settlement expanded, new militia companies were organized in the various new localities. In 1630, two military instructors were recruited and, from July 1631, these drilled on the first Friday of every month with the militiamen from Charlestown company.[25] Musketeers carried muskets, bandoliers with bullet bags and swords; they could also have a helmet instead of the normal hat. Pikemen had helmets, breast and back plates of armour with tassets, pikes and swords. Usually, in a militia company, there were two musketeers for every pikeman. Captains and lieutenants were armed with partizans, while sergeants had halberds. Each company had drummers and ensigns who carried the company's colours. In general terms, as in nearby Plymouth colony, the English Trained Band system was copied accurately and adopted by the colonial militias. In March 1631, the colonial authorities in Boston ordered that all able-bodied men living in the city should be furnished with good and sufficient weapons for defence of the settlement: these had to be provided by the city's government if the individual could not afford them.[26]

During the period October–December 1636, the militia companies of Massachusetts Bay colony were reordered and formed into three regiments: the East, North and South Regiments, under command of Colonels John Winthrop, John Haynes and John Endecott. The East Regiment was the most important one, including militia companies from Boston, Roxburry, Dorchester, Weymouth and Hingham. Despite this new organization, there were still many independent 'Trainband' companies in the outlying communities. According to a document dating back to 1638, the militiamen serving in the three regiments had to be equipped as follows: light armour, musket (having a 5ft barrel), sword, bandolier, belt and ammunition.[27] It was acceptable if half of the men had armour, so long as all had muskets and swords. In 1643, the general organization was changed again, with the creation of new county regiments that bore the names of their respective counties. With the general growth in the number of militia units, there was a new need for specialized training. As a result, during 1637, there were proposals to set up in Boston a unit to provide training for militia officers and artillery services. The idea was that of creating something similar to the City of London's 'Artillery Garden', which later became known as the 'Honourable Artillery Company'.[28] On 13 March 1638, the colonial authorities granted a charter for creation of 'The Military Company of Massachusetts', whose first commander was the veteran Captain Robert Keayne

---

[24] Ibid., p.4.
[25] Ibid.
[26] Ibid.
[27] Ibid., p.5.
[28] Ibid.

'The North Regiment from Massachusetts Bay Colony 1636–1637', by H. Charles McBarron, *MUIA Pl. 61*, © The Company of Military Historians.

'New England Independent Companies 1675–1676', by Eric Manders, *MUIA Pl. 244*, © The Company of Military Historians.

(who had served in the London Company). Under Keayne's guidance, the new company became the first military training unit and the first artillery school of the American colonies. Many of the future militia officers underwent their initial training in the ranks of the Massachusetts Company. As in the rest of the other North American colonies, Massachusetts cavalry appeared only at a later date: around 1650, when horses were becoming increasingly common in Massachusetts colony, a troop of horses was formed. Originally, the members of this unit were militiamen who acted as mounted soldiers only when their own county regiment was not in exercise.[29] During the following years more troops of horses were formed; by 1667 there were twelve, with 160 cavalrymen each. Each trooper, like the foot militiamen, was to furnish arms and equipment for himself (in addition to his horse). Apparently, these mounted militiamen had excellent equipment (including buff coats, pistols, hangers and corselets) and proved to be very useful during the military operations of King Philip's War.

In 1667, Massachusetts' militia strength was estimated at 30,000 able-bodied men, aged between 16 and 60. These trained eight times each year; in addition, each town had some artillerymen who trained every week. By 1676, the Massachusetts militia had notably expanded and could mobilize up to 40,000 able-bodied men (4,000 of them alone in Boston). The trained bands numbered 6,000 of the best-equipped infantry, which by now included no pikemen.[30] Most of the bands and the other militia units were located in the Boston area, as were the main fortifications. In late 1675, when King Philip launched his assaults against the colonies of New England, Massachusetts – together with Plymouth colony – mobilized 700 infantrymen and 200 horsemen. The foot militiamen were grouped into the provisional Massachusetts Regiment and took part in the bloody Great Swamp Fight. In 1676, the Boston Militia Regiment, which had been structured on four companies until then, was doubled to eight companies. In the following decades, as a result of the emergency faced during King Philip's War, the Massachusetts militia continued to expand as the colony grew, with more county regiments being formed. Regimental musters were held only once every three years, except in Boston. Officers were usually chosen by the men of their companies, with their names submitted to the General Assembly of the colony for approval.[31] According to the 1693 Militia Act, the personal equipment of each militiaman should include musket, cartouche box and sword; as always, sergeants carried halberds. During King William's War and Queen Anne's War, the county militia regiments formed the pool of men from which volunteer temporary units were raised for expeditions.

---

[29] Ibid., p.6.
[30] Ibid.
[31] Ibid.

Chapter 8

Bacon's Rebellion

The Royal colony of Virginia

I n 1624, the Virginia Company's charter was revoked and the colony transferred to royal authority as a crown colony, but the elected representatives in Jamestown continued to exercise a good amount of power over the settlement. Ten years later, in 1634, a new system of local government was created by order of King Charles I: eight shires were designated, each with its own local officers; these shires were renamed as counties only a few years later. Now under direct royal authority, the colony began to expand to the north and west with the building of additional settlements. The first significant attempts at exploring the Trans-Allegheny region took place under the administration of Governor William Berkeley.[1] However, further exploring expeditions were blocked in 1644 when about 500 colonists were killed in another Indian massacre: like the previous one of 1622, this one was led by Opechanacanough and resulted in the Third Anglo-Powhatan War.

In July 1644, the Virginia militiamen marched against the main Indian villages and severely defeated the forces of Opechanacanough. In February 1645, three new frontier forts were built for protection against any future Indian raid: Fort Charles at the falls of the James River, Fort James on the Chickahominy and Fort Royal at the falls of the York River. In August, Governor Berkeley stormed Opechanacanough's main stronghold and captured him. The Indian chief, by then around 92 years old, was taken to Jamestown, where he was shot in the back by a guard. The events of 1644–1645 resulted in the final disintegration of the Powhatan Confederacy into various smaller tribes, attacked by the English colonists in the following years.[2] In March 1646, a fourth frontier fort, Fort Henry, was built at the falls of the Appomattox River (on the site where the modern city of Petersburg is now located). Finally, in October 1646, the English and the Powhatan Indians came to an agreement and a treaty was signed between the two parts. According to it, the various sub-tribes formerly part of the Powhatan Confederacy became tributaries to the King of England. At the same time, a precise racial frontier was established along the English and Indian territories: to enter the territory of Virginia colony, Indians had to obtain a special pass from one of the newly erected border forts.[3] In addition, the treaty of 1646 gave a lot of new territories to Virginia colony, especially between the James and Blackwater rivers and on the peninsula north of the York and below the Poropotank rivers. During the English Civil War, most of the colonists

---

[1]   Tisdale, D. A., *Soldiers of the Virginia Colony, 1607–1699*, Petersburg, 2000.
[2]   Pieroni, Piero, *I grandi capi Indiani*, Florence, 1963, p. 70.
[3]   Ibid., p.72.

in Virginia remained loyal to the king, as well as Governor Berkeley. In 1652, however, Oliver Cromwell sent a small military force to remove and replace him with Richard Bennett, who was loyal to the Commonwealth of England. The new governor was a moderate Puritan and allowed the local legislature to exercise most controlling authority. He was followed by two more 'Cromwellian' governors, Edward Digges and Samuel Matthews. After the Restoration, in recognition for Virginia's loyalty to the crown, King Charles II bestowed the colony with the nickname 'The Old Dominion'.

The revolt

In 1660, following the Restoration in England, William Berkeley was again made Governor of Virginia. In many respects, his second period of rule proved to be less positive than his first: his new dismissive policy was not the right way to face the political challenges of Virginia's western frontiers. Many colonists wished to push westward to claim Indian frontier land, but in this they were actively countered by the measures ordered by Governor Berkeley. Following a raid by the Indians in Stafford County, a group of Virginia militiamen led by Nathaniel Bacon raided some native settlements across the Potomac River in Maryland; these actions

Governor Berkeley baring his breast for Bacon to shoot after refusing him the requested military commission. Public domain picture obtained from Wikimedia Commons.

were conducted with no official authorisation from the governor. The Governor of Maryland officially protested against the incursion, but some militiamen from his colony joined Virginia forces and continued the punitive campaign against the Indians. The combined militia forces attacked a fortified native village and later killed five Indian chiefs during a parley.[4] As a result, the Indians retaliated in force against the English plantations, both in Virginia and Maryland. Around 100 settlers were killed and many houses or fields were burned as far as the James and York Rivers. Seeking to avoid a large Indian conflict similar to King Philip's War, Berkeley advocated containment and proposed the construction of several defensive fortifications along the frontier. Frontier settlers criticized this plan as expensive and inadequate, questioning it as a possible excuse to raise tax rates and augment corruption. Many Virginian farmers gathered to protest against the governor's decision. They also protested against corruption in the colonial government, which caused widespread inefficiency. Bacon soon became the leader of the protesting freeholders; he was the owner of two large frontier plantations on the James River and lived in Jamestown. His cousin was a prominent militia colonel and a personal friend of the governor: as a result, shortly after his arrival in America, Bacon had been appointed to the governor's council. His main objective was that of enlarging his personal possessions by conquering new lands from the Indians. It is quite probable, however, that his real ambition was that of replacing Berkeley as governor of the colony. Bacon mustered a force of 400–500 militiamen and moved up the James River to attack the Indians, with no authorization to do so.[5] When he and his men came back to Jamestown, they discovered that Berkeley had been forced to call for new elections to the House of Burgesses. Despite his outlaw status, Bacon had been elected, but when he attempted to take his seat, Berkeley had him arrested. Soon released by his men, Bacon gathered his supporters and marched on Jamestown.

After some resistance, Berkeley was coerced to sign the military commission for war against the Indians that Bacon demanded. After doing this, he abandoned Jamestown and went to his plantations, leaving Bacon in complete control of the House of Burgesses. Under Bacon's guidance, the latter enacted a series of sweeping reforms which limited the governor's powers and restored suffrage rights to landless freemen. On 30 July 1676, Bacon issued a 'Declaration of the People of Virginia', which criticized Berkeley's administration by accusing him of levying unfair taxes and appointing friends to high positions. He also issued a 'Manifesto' which urged the extermination of all the Indians living on the frontiers of Virginia. Months of civil strife ensued, with Bacon's men also fighting against the Indians. Meanwhile, from his properties in the east of Virginia, Governor Berkeley gathered enough supporters to return to Jamestown, including a large number of mercenaries. Back in his capital, the governor proclaimed Bacon and his men rebels and traitors. Berkeley's victory, however, was not to last for long: after a short skirmish, Bacon recaptured Jamestown and obliged the governor to flee again. Fearing that he could not hold the city against Berkeley's counter-attack, Bacon decided to set fire to Jamestown on 19 September 1676, burning it to

---

4   Ibid.
5   Tisdale, D.A., *Soldiers of the Virginia Colony, 1607–1699* (Petersburg, 2000).

The burning of Jamestown by Bacon and his forces. Public domain picture obtained from Wikimedia Commons.

the ground. Now controlling most of Virginia's territory, Bacon died suddenly on 26 October 1676. John Ingram took over leadership of the rebellion, but many followers drifted away. Berkeley launched a series of successful amphibious attacks across Chesapeake Bay and defeated the rebels in various skirmishes. Without Bacon's strong leadership, the rebellion soon collapsed, even before the arrival of the English regular troops sent by King Charles II to suppress the revolt. Governor Berkeley wreaked a bloody vengeance, seizing the properties of several rebels and hanging some of them without a regular trial. After an investigative committee returned its report to King Charles II, criticizing Berkeley for his conduct, the old governor was relieved of his functions and ordered to return in England. Bacon's Rebellion was the first revolt in the North American colonies in which discontented colonists took part, exactly 100 years before the beginning of the American Revolution.

The military organization of Virginia, 1635–1713

In April 1644, the Third Anglo-Powhatan War broke out, completely surprising the Virginia colonists. The hard-pressed colonial authorities struggled to restore order and prepared the militia for the defence of the territory. During June, offensive operations against the Indians began and a force of 300 militiamen led by William Clairborne was formed. Every man of this small army had to carry musket, black powder, ammunition, defensive coat or armour, helmet, sword or cutlass and food provisions for three weeks.[6] Clairborne's militiamen were effective in burning Indian villages and crops, thus stopping the raids of the natives, but this provisional force was disbanded in August. Now having the initiative, small parties of Virginia militiamen continued to destroy Indian crops during the following months. In 1645, more parties of militiamen were sent out to launch raids against the natives, including some newly formed mounted patrols. In 1646, a small force of just sixty militiamen, well-armed with guns, swords and bullet bags, pursued and captured the Powhatan chief Opechanacanough.[7]

In the years following the last Anglo-Powhatan War, the number of militia companies increased as the colony grew and new counties were created to administer the settlements. Since 1651, the militia companies were assembled into county regiments. In 1664, as a result of the arrival of the Dutch fleet in North America, the colonial authorities of Virginia raised a force of 2,500 infantrymen and 1,500 cavalrymen to patrol the coasts of the colony.[8] In those years, the military government of Virginia was divided into four provinces, one being under the governor and the other three under major-generals of the militia. Each county within a province had a regiment of foot and a troop of horses; in total, the territory of Virginia included nineteen counties. In addition to the militia forces, the governor also had a small personal guard that was commanded by a commissioned captain of the guard.[9] During Bacon's Rebellion, part of the militia supported the popular leader in his rising against the autocratic Governor William Berkeley. In the ensuing civil strife, the militia units fought on opposing sides until Berkeley was able to suppress the rebellion. Meanwhile, however,

[6]   Chartrand, René, *Colonial American Troops 1610–1774 (1)* (Oxford, 2002), p.36.
[7]   Ibid.
[8]   Ibid.
[9]   Ibid.

English sergeant, early seventeenth century. Public domain picture from the Vinkhuijzen Collection of military uniforms, part of the New York Public Library digital collections.

King James II had sent a regular unit to Virginia in order to crush the rebels: the so-called Jeffery's Regiment. When this unit went back to England, two independent companies of English regulars were formed to remain as a garrison in Virginia. As a result, most of the garrison duties were taken up by these royal troops; this situation, however, was not to last for long. Following the disbandment of the two regular companies in May 1682, militiamen were again employed to garrison the frontier forts. By 1684, however, the colonial authorities had serious difficulties in finding the required militiamen to perform garrison duties. During this period, the small parties which garrisoned the frontier forts (numbering around thirty men each) started to be composed of mounted militiamen known as rangers. These horsemen were a mounted patrol keeping watch along the line of forts rather than cavalry in the European tactical sense: in practice, they were a sort of mounted infantry.[10] Nor were they the woods-running elite light infantry created by Benjamin Church. They were paid in tobacco and had to provide their own arms, clothing, equipment, saddlery and horses. The general militia, meanwhile, maintained its county organization during the following decades, with some units being particularly well appointed (especially some troops of horse). In 1702, with the outbreak of Queen Anne's War, the colonial authorities of Virginia received arms for 1,000 infantrymen and 400 cavalrymen; however, the colony was not practically involved in the military operations of the war.[11]

---

[10] Ibid., p.37.
[11] Ibid.

Chapter 9

The growth of New France

After the foundation of the first stable settlements, Samuel de Champlain – first Governor of New France – arranged to have young Frenchmen live with the local natives, in order to learn their language and customs. These men, known as '*coureurs des bois*' (literally meaning 'runners of the woods'), adapted very soon to the harsh life of North America and gradually extended French influence south and west to the Great Lakes and among the powerful Huron tribes living there. During the first decades of the colony's existence, the French population in Canada numbered only a few hundred, while the English colonies to the south were already much more populous and wealthy. Cardinal Richelieu, at that time adviser to King Louis XIII, had the ambition to make New France as significant and rich as the English colonies. For this reason, in 1627, he founded the Company of the One Hundred Associates to invest in Canada, promising land parcels to hundreds of new settlers in order to turn New France into an important mercantile and farming colony. Champlain was named Governor of New France and Richelieu forbade non-Roman Catholics from living there. This was a great mistake, because many of the best elements of French society, who were abandoning France as a result of the religious persecutions, had to emigrate to other countries. Many French Protestants (Huguenots) went to the English North American colonies, thus depriving Canada of a great community of potential settlers. Regarding administration of the new territories, Richelieu introduced the so-called 'seigneurial' system, a semi-feudal system of farming that remained a characteristic feature of the St Lawrence River Valley for a long time.

During the 1630s, the Roman Catholic Church became firmly established in the new Canadian colonies, mainly thanks to the presence and efforts of the Jesuits. After Champlain's death in 1634, the French Church soon became a dominant power of New France. The Jesuits, in particular, were the driving element of this process: during the 1640s, several Jesuit missionaries penetrated the Great Lakes region and converted many of the local Huron Indians. In 1642, the French Church sponsored a group of colonists who founded the settlement of Ville-Marie, precursor to present-day Montreal, further up the St Lawrence River. Very soon the presence of Jesuit missionaries in Huron society became essential: the Indians totally relied on French goods for both daily life and warfare.[1] Because the French would refuse trade to all tribes denying relations with the missionaries, the Hurons had more of a propensity towards Christian conversion. With the growing epidemics and subsequent high number of deaths, the Hurons could not afford to lose relations with the French. Many of the Indian conversions were thus the result of the Hurons' fear of epidemics: many natives, in fact,

---

[1]   Pieroni, Piero, *I grandi capi Indiani* (Florence, 1963), p.101.

Canadian '*coureurs des bois*' meeting with friendly Indians. Public domain picture obtained from Wikimedia Commons.

believed that if they did not convert to Christianity they would be exposed to the evil magic of the French priests, which caused the illness.[2] Around the middle of the century, however, both the system of Jesuit missions and the Hurons were almost destroyed by the Iroquois invasions.

The English conquest of Quebec and Acadia

After less than twenty years of French presence, the Canadian colonies were already flourishing and showed a great potential for future developments. Being aware of this, the English colonial authorities in the south started to plan some military moves to counter French expansionism. English privateers began to launch raids in the St Lawrence River Valley, and in 1629, Quebec City itself was captured and held by the English until 1632. This English capture of Quebec is one of the least-known military events in the history of Canada, but it proved to be a real threat to the survival of the French colonies in North America. Everything

---

[2]   Ibid.

began two years before, in 1627, when several London merchants formed the Company of Merchant Adventurers with the objective of developing trade and settlement on the St Lawrence River. Made up of private investors, it was chartered as usual by the Crown, as a means of extending English influence in Canada and dislodging the French from their new colonies. Later that year, the Company financed an armed expedition to expel the French settlers from Canada, which was commissioned by King Charles I of England. The expedition was led by David Kirke and included three ships. Before arriving at Quebec, the English privateers seized a supply ship that was directed to the French colony and sent some Basque fishermen as emissaries to the Governor of New France, Samuel de Champlain. Champlain rejected demands to surrender the fortesss town because he was waiting for a relief force coming from France and was confident of its imminent arrival. Knowing this, Kirke decided not to attack the city and set sail for England. On their way home, however, the English ships met the French supply fleet of four ships that Champlain was waiting for. The Englishmen attacked the French ships and, after a brief naval battle, captured all of them. Kirke's expedition had not conquered Quebec City, but the capture of a French fleet was considered a great success when the privateers returned to England.

In 1629, the Company of Merchant Adventurers organized a second expedition against New France, this time with the firm determination to assault Quebec. The English invasion fleet, this time including six ships and three pinnaces, departed in March, with a French deserter acting as pilot. Kirke, this time aware of the desperate conditions of Quebec's military defences, again demanded the surrender of the city after his arrival in July. Champlain, having no alternative and no possibility to attempt a defence, surrendered Quebec on 19 July. Impressed by this achievement, members of the Company soon applied to the Crown for letters patent to give them the sole right to trade and settle in Canada along the St Lawrence River. But all these projects soon proved to be an illusion: when the English expedition had departed from Europe, France and England were at war, but by the time Quebec was conquered, the two countries had already agreed a peace treaty. As a result, Kirke's occupation of Quebec City was illegal. Starting from this legal assumption, Champlain worked in the following years for restitution of New France to the legitimate settlers. As part of the ongoing peace negotiations, King Charles I of England agreed to return Quebec to France in 1632, in exchange for Louis XIII paying his wife's dowry.

While all this was happening along the St Lawrence River, the French colony in Acadia in the Gulf of St Lawrence was occupied by a small group of Scottish colonists. In 1629, Sir James Stewart of Killeith planted a colony on Cape Breton Island at Baleine, while Sir William Alexander established the first settlement of a New Scotland colony by conquering Port-Royal from the few French colonists. In 1621, King James I of England had granted to Alexander all of Acadia, which was known by the English colonists as Nova Scotia; eight years later, seventy Scottish colonists were finally able to occupy the settlement. In the following years, these also organized a militia of some sort. However, Scottish colonization of the Americas lasted for only a few years: similarly to what happened to Quebec City, Acadia was returned to the French in 1632 under the terms of the Saint Germain–en–Laye peace treaty between England and France. In the following years the French reinforced their fortifications

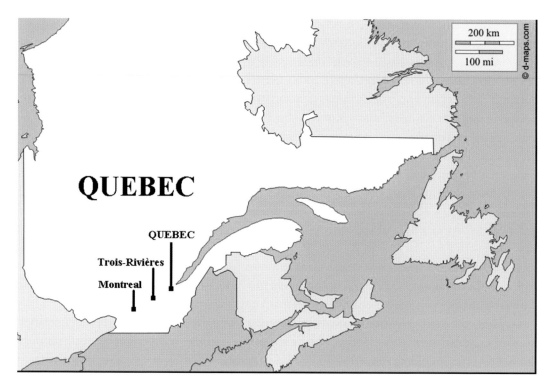

Map of Quebec, with the location of the main French settlements along the St Lawrence River. Map modified by Gabriele Esposito; original obtained from http://d-maps.com/carte.php?num_car=1872&lang=en.

in Acadia, especially at Port-Royal: by now it was clear to them that the English had a strong interest in the region.

The Beaver Wars and the fall of Huronia

By the 1630s, the Iroquois had become fully armed with European weaponry through their flourishing trade with the Dutch settlers at Fort Orange.[3] The Mohawks, in particular, had come to rely on the trade for firearms and other highly valued European goods for their own livelihood and survival.[4] As time progressed, the Iroquois started to use their growing expertise with European firearms in their long wars against rival tribes such as the Algonquin, Mohicans, Montagnais and Hurons. Although the Iroquois first attacked their traditional native enemies, the alliance of these tribes with the French quickly brought the Iroquois into fierce and bloody conflict against the colonists. The expansion of hunting for the fur trade with the Europeans accelerated the decline of the beaver population in the regions inhabited

---

[3]   Johnson, Michael G., *Tribes of the Iroquois Confederacy* (Oxford, 2003).
[4]   Pieroni, Piero, *I grandi capi Indiani* (Florence, 1963), p.103.

by the Iroquois: by 1640, the beaver had largely disappeared from the Hudson River Valley.[5]
The growing scarcity of this precious animal was the main cause that accelerated the outbreak of hostilities between the Iroquois and the colonists of New France.[6] In those years the
centre of the fur trade was gradually shifting northward to the colder regions of present-day
southern Ontario, an area which was mainly inhabited by the Hurons. As we have seen, these
were allies and close trading partners of the French. The Iroquois, feeling threatened by their
high losses to smallpox and other infectious diseases, began an aggressive campaign against
the Hurons and the French to expand their hunting areas. In 1638, they attacked the Wenro
Indians and occupied all their territory, mainly thanks to the use of superior European weaponry. After the defeat, Wenro survivors fled to the Hurons for refuge; for a long time the
Wenro tribe had served as a buffer between the Iroquois and the Hurons.[7] Now, with expansion to the west blocked by the presence of the European settlements, the Iroquois could only
continue their advance towards the north. In this they were encouraged by the Dutch, who
continued to furnish them with weapons and military provisions. The French, instead, generally refused to sell or exchange firearms with the Indians; weapons were sometimes given
only to Hurons converted to Christianity. The smouldering conflict between the Iroquois
and the French finally erupted in 1641, when New France's Governor Montmagny went
by boat to a meeting with the Iroquois chiefs near Trois-Rivières, in order to negotiate with
them. When the colonists arrived at the meeting, the Indians attacked them with arrows. The
French responded with musket fire and any hope for a peace treaty was virtually cancelled in
those few minutes.

If the inhabitants of Quebec City lived in relative security, the same was not true for the
other French settlements, like Trois-Rivières or Montreal. As a result, the colonial authorities had to start a general improvement of New France's defensive system. In August 1642,
Governor Montmagny ordered the construction of a fort at the mouth of the Richelieu River,
the main function of which was blocking the traditional invasion route of the Iroquois.[8] Later
that year, the new fort was attacked by the Indians: their skill in handling firearms surprised
the French defenders, who were very few and suffered from a severe lack of supply. The
Iroquois maintained a constant state of guerrilla warfare, killing any soldier who tried to venture outside the fortification. As a result, the small fort was practically under siege until it was
finally abandoned toward the end of 1646. Some months later it was burned by the Iroquois
warriors. To help their Indian allies, the French had also sent a small group of soldiers to the
Hurons during the winter of 1643–1644, in order to protect the missions of the Jesuits that
were located on the frontier with the Iroquois. In the spring of 1649, the Iroquois launched
their final assault against the Hurons, with the declared objectives of destroying them and
conquering all of their territories. More than 1,000 Iroquois warriors, very well armed with
modern firearms, descended on Huronia. Several Huron villages, as well as the Jesuit mis-

---

5   Johnson, Michael G., *Tribes of the Iroquois Confederacy* (Oxford, 2003).
6   Pieroni, Piero, *I grandi capi Indiani* (Florence, 1963), p.103.
7   Ibid.
8   Chartrand, René, *Canadian Military Heritage (Volume 1, 1000–1754)* (Montreal, 1993), p.54.

French colonist and allied Indians fighting against the Iroquois. Public domain picture obtained from Wikimedia Commons.

sions of Saint-Louis and Saint-Ignace, fell to the invaders. After this advance, the French also decided to abandon the most important mission of the region, that of Sainte-Marie. Huronia had been conquered by the Iroquois: the few surviving French and Hurons who fled from the region took refuge on Christian Island. During the summer, the refugees tried to fortify the island in preparation for an Iroquois attack; in the following winter, however, famine struck the new little colony. As a result, on 10 June 1650, the few remaining Frenchmen and Hurons set out for Quebec City.

Indian guerrillas

The fall of Huronia enabled the Iroquois to concentrate all their following war efforts against the French settlements of the St Lawrence River Valley. The French concentrated their forces and abandoned all the missions or commercial posts that were located west of Montreal. As a result of this strategic retreat, all the major routes to Montreal came under control of the Iroquois: the Ottawa River, Richelieu River and upper St Lawrence River. Indian incursions and raids increased in number and intensity, causing a continuous state of guerrilla war-fare between Iroquois war parties and the French settlements. Unlike the colonists of New England and New Netherland in the south, the French ones had to face the Indians in the heart of their territories, with terrible results for the productive and economic life of New France. In 1653, the two parties concluded a peace treaty and suspended hostilities, but this was not to last for long. During this small period of peace, in July 1656, the French built a Jesuit mission in the heart of the Iroquois territory. The desire to have a mission on their ter-ritory had been expressed by the Onondaga nation three years before, but not all the Iroquois tribes were favourable to the establishment of a French presence on their territory.[9] The Mohawks, in particular, launched a series of raids against the new mission of Sainte-Marie, with the objective of breaking the peace treaty with the French. In the autumn of 1657, the situation became gradually impossible to sustain for the French, as the Indian raids started to involve a wider area than previously. On 20 March 1658, the mission was secretly abandoned under the cover of darkness.

War with the Iroquois broke out once again, this time with an even higher level of inten-sity and violence. During the few years of relative peace with the French, the Iroquois had defeated their traditional enemies to the west and thus had nothing more to fear from other Indian tribes.[10] Always well provided with weapons by the Dutch, the Iroquois went from victory to victory for nearly a decade. They attacked everywhere, being able to disappear immediately thanks to their elusive tactics.[11] The French tried to respond to this kind of warfare, but no significant victory was achieved, at least for the moment. In 1658, Governor Vover d'Argenson set off in pursuit of the Iroquois with a party of 100 men. His intention was to oblige the Iroquois to fight in a conventional pitched battle against his well-drilled European soldiers, which he had every expectation of winning.[12] In the end the expedition proved to be a failure because the French soldiers were not able to intercept the Indians and the planned field battle never took place. The military initiative was always in the hands of the Iroquois because the colonists received practically no help from France, despite all their desperate appeals for assistance. The ambitious d'Argenson was thus obliged to adopt only defensive measures, for example encouraging the inhabitants to avoid living in isolation and instead gather together in fortified settlements. This was the most difficult period in the

---

[9]   Ibid., p.57.
[10] Johnson, Michael G., *Tribes of the Iroquois Confederacy* (Oxford, 2003).
[11] Chartrand, René, *Canadian Military Heritage (Volume 1, 1000–1754)* (Montreal, 1993), p.58.
[12] Ibid.

history of New France: the colonists gradually succumbed to a siege mentality, and even the windmills were fortified.[13]

The Acadian civil war

While the French settlements in the St Lawrence River Valley were at war with the Iroquois, the colony of Acadia was involved in a civil war between competing governors, something that had never happened before in New France. In 1625, Charles de Saint-Étienne de La Tour built a new fort, named Fort Pentagouet, in present-day Castine (Maine), near a site where a French trading post had been established as early as 1613. In 1631, he also fortified a strategic location at the mouth of the Saint John River, where a new fortification named Fort Sainte Marie was built. In 1635, Governor of Acadia Charles de Menou d'Aulnay moved some set-tlers from present-day LaHave to Port-Royal and the Acadian colonists began to establish their roots. Under d'Aulnay, the Acadian settlers built the first dykes of North America and cultivated salt marshes. In the following years, the French settlement started to flourish, thanks to its good levels of productivity. During the years 1640–1645, war broke out between the legitimate Governor d'Aulnay and La Tour. The former was based in Port-Royal, while the latter had his stronghold at Fort Pentagouet. Both d'Aulnay and La Tour had claims of some legitimacy to the governorship of Acadia, because La Tour's settlement was not clearly defined as a dependency of d'Aulnay's main colony at Port-Royal. In nearby New England, the English colonists supported La Tour's claims because he allowed them to fish and lumber in and along the Bay of Fundy; d'Aulnay, instead, aggressively sought payment for those same rights. As time progressed, the contrasting ambitions of the two competing governors became incompatible: when word came to La Tour that d'Aulnay was concentrating men and materials for an attack on his fort and fur trading base at the mouth of the Saint John River, he went to Boston to ask for help from the English Massachusetts Bay colony. Governor John Winthrop gave no direct help, but arranged for several English merchants to advance loans unofficially to La Tour, which were to be used for recruiting of mercenaries and purchasing of materials. The main objective of the English colonial authorities was preventing d'Aulnay from capturing the fortified settlement on the mouth of the Saint John River, in order to maintain the fishing privileges that they had acquired thanks to La Tour.

   With the help of the Massachusetts merchants, La Tour was able to organize an expedition with two armed ships in 1640 and attacked Port-Royal. The assault was repulsed and thus the military initiative passed into the hands of d'Aulnay. The latter sailed out of Port-Royal and established a blockade of La Tour's fort. In 1642, for five months, d'Aulnay blockaded the Saint John River in order to obtain the surrender of La Tour's defensive position. On 14 July 1643, however, La Tour arrived at the head of a relief expedition from Boston, with four ships and 270 men. He repulsed the enemy forces and broke the blockade. After this victory, he chased d'Aulnay's vessels back across the Bay of Fundy to attack the main colony of Port-Royal. La Tour burned the mill, killed the livestock and seized furs, gunpowder and other

---

13   Ibid., p.59.

supplies. Despite these losses, d'Aulnay resisted the attack and was able to maintain possession of Port-Royal. On 13 April 1645, while La Tour was in Boston to recruit new military
forces, d'Aulnay sailed across the Bay of Fundy and arrived at La Tour's fort with a force of
around 200 men. After a fierce fight that lasted for five days, d'Aulnay offered quarter to all
the defenders of the fort if they would surrender. The besieged accepted this generous offer
and Fort Sainte-Marie was finally captured. D'Aulnay then reneged on his pledge of safety
for the defenders and treacherously hanged the captured garrison of the fort. With the loss of
his fort, La Tour took refuge in Quebec and did not return to Acadia for the next four years,
until after d'Aulnay died in 1650. The governorship of Acadia was now open and, in 1653, La
Tour married d'Aulnay's widow, thus ending the long rivalry. The destiny of Acadia, however,
also proved to be turbulent in the following years. In 1654, Colonel Robert Sedgewick led
100 New England volunteers and 200 regular soldiers to capture Port-Royal and the whole
territory of Acadia. Before the final battle at Port-Royal, Sedgewick captured and plundered
Governor La Tour's fort on the Saint John River and took him prisoner. Acadia was returned
to the French only in 1667 by the Treaty of Breda, but actual repossession did not occur
until three years later, when Massachusetts militia abandoned the territory and a new French
governor arrived. In 1674, while France was at war with the Netherlands, a Dutch privateer
showed up in Acadian waters to attack the French settlement. At that time there were no
French ships in the area and the forts were defended by very small garrisons: as a result, some
French positions were taken and pillaged by the Dutch, who even captured the local governor
and his officers before abandoning Acadia. Despite the losses suffered during this assault,
Acadia remained practically undefended until the 1680s.

The Battle of Long Sault and the turning point of the Iroquois Wars

In the spring of 1660, Adam Dollard des Ormeaux, the young commander of the Montreal
garrison, left the city at the head of an expedition numbering just sixteen men. The small
group headed north-west up the Ottawa River, with the objective of protecting a convoy of
furs coming from the Ottawa Valley. When Dollard's group arrived at an abandoned fort at
Long Sault, it was joined by a number of Indian allies (mostly Hurons). Totally unexpect-
edly, another group of Indian warriors appeared: this time, however, the newcomers were not
friendly natives but 200 Iroquois. These were as surprised to find the French at Long Sault as
Dollard's men were to see them.[14] The Iroquois party attacked the French immediately, but
were repulsed; as a result, some of the warriors canoed to the Richelieu River to seek reinforcements from the Mohawks and Oneidas living in the area. Very soon the Iroquois tribes
were able to send strong reinforcements to Long Sault, including a number of 'Iroquoized'
Hurons. The latter, after arriving on the field of battle, convinced thirty of the Indians fighting
with the French to abandon them and join their native brothers.[15] Meanwhile, Dollard's men
and the remaining allied natives entered the abandoned fort in order to attempt a desperate

---

[14]   Ibid.
[15]   Ibid., p.60.

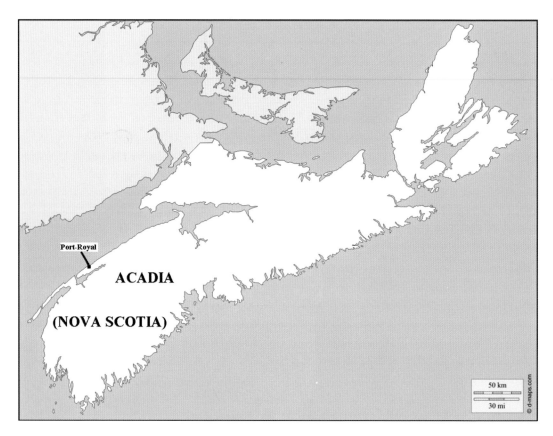

Map of French Acadia (later British Nova Scotia) with the location of Port Royal. Map modified by Gabriele Esposito; original obtained from http://d-maps.com/carte.php?num_car=23338&lang=en.

final defence. The Iroquois launched a general assault, but they were again repulsed. At this point the attackers tried to knock down the palisade of the fortification and threw an entire powder keg inside the fort. The result of this action was catastrophic for the French, most of whom were killed by the ensuing explosion. Only five Frenchmen and four Hurons survived, but they were killed shortly after during the subsequent final attack of the Iroquois. The clash at Long Sault had been another serious defeat for the French, but luckily for them the Iroquois warriors preferred to return home instead of launching a new offensive against Montreal.[16]

In the spring of 1661, the Iroquois raids against New France resumed with even greater intensity, with about 100 colonists being killed. The situation for the French colonies, however, was finally going to change in a definitive way. The incessant requests of help coming from Canada started to be seriously considered in France, with the result that the Company of the Hundred Associates agreed to send 100 soldiers as reinforcements for New France. These arrived at the same time as the new Governor Pierre Du Bois D'Avaugour, an experienced

---

[16] Johnson, Michael G., *Tribes of the Iroquois Confederacy* (Oxford, 2003).

military commander who had served under Turenne. It was soon clear to him, however, that 100 soldiers were not enough to face the Iroquois in an effective way. In 1662, the raids of the Indians continued to cause problems: as a response, another 100 soldiers were sent from France, together with a large amount of goods and ammunition. This was still not enough, but the royal court and government in France were now aware of the dramatic Canadian situation.[17] At that time, in fact, there was a new-found royal interest in the colonies, and New France in particular. By 1660, the French colonies in America still had many difficulties, being neither rich nor developed like those of New England or New Netherland; they struggled to get by and remained on a virtually perpetual war footing because of the Iroquois.[18] While the English colonies counted 90,000 inhabitants and the smaller New Netherland 10,000, Canada had just 3,500 colonists and a very small military garrison. Significant steps needed to be taken if New France was to flourish and expand like the other European colonies. Luckily for the colonists of Canada, a strong military response arrived in the following years.

The Carignan-Salières Regiment in New France

When Cardinal Mazarin died in March 1661, the young King Louis XIV started to govern by himself and took over control of France and the colonial possessions. As a result, a great wave of significant reforms swept through all French institutions, especially in the army. In 1663, the king and his ministers turned to the colonial problem. The first step that needed to be taken was breaking the monopoly of the trading companies and substituting it with royal authority. In order to replace the old private companies, the new Companies of the East and West Indies were established. Unlike the previous ones, these companies were creatures of the king: the state treasury joined forces with private capital, the king's navy escorted merchant ships and the monarch started to exercise considerable control over the colonial settlements.[19] For the first time in French military history, regular troops were detached from the royal army to serve overseas. It was Canada that received the most significant benefits from this new colonial policy. In the summer of 1665, an entire infantry regiment numbering 1,000 men was sent to New France: the Carignan-Salières Regiment would soon achieve almost legendary status. With the arrival of such a significant military force, the balance of power in Canada changed completely. By the end of August 1665, eight companies of the regiment had already been sent to build new strongholds all along the Richelieu River. Towns and settlements were by now defended with suitable garrisons, and new forts were constructed to block the traditional invasion paths of the Iroquois. In a few weeks New France, which had been struggling for its survival for a quarter of a century, transformed its military role from that of being besieged to that of an expansionist aggressor. In January 1666, some 300 soldiers from the Carignan Salières Regiment plus

---

[17] Chartrand, René, *Canadian Military Heritage (Volume 1, 1000–1754)* (Montreal, 1993), p.62.
[18] Ibid.
[19] Ibid., p.63.

English officer, late sixteenth century. Public domain picture from the Vinkhuijzen Collection of military uniforms, part of the New York Public Library digital collections.

French arquebusier, late sixteenth century. Public domain picture from the Vinkhuijzen Collection of military uniforms, part of the New York Public Library digital collections.

200 Canadian volunteers, under guidance of Governor de Courcelles, left Quebec City and marched against the Iroquois territory. This operation was an astonishing undertaking, because no European military force in North America had ever launched a winter offensive against the Indians. During their march, the French soldiers were joined by further volunteers coming from Montreal. This first expedition of the Carignan-Salières Regiment eventually proved a total fiasco, because no Iroquois village was destroyed. However, it had radically changed the mentality of the Canadian military forces forever.[20] The French learned many lessons from this large-scale winter expedition, conducted in one of the world's most hostile environments.

During the spring and summer of 1666, various skirmishes were fought between the French and Iroquois. In July, a force of 200 French soldiers and volunteers, together with eighty native allies, approached an Iroquois village to attack it. The Indians sent out a peace envoy and liberated a few French captives, fearing that a French attack would destroy their village. When the expedition returned to Quebec, the colonial authorities became convinced that Iroquois territory could easily be penetrated. Weary of the ineffectual peace negotiations that were going on with the Iroquois and of the continuous minor raids, the French decided to launch a major and decisive expedition to end the war. In September 1666, a small army of 700 soldiers, 400 Canadian volunteers and 100 Indian allies marched to the very heart of the Iroquois territory. The Iroquois hid in the forests and offered no resistance to the French, even when the invaders burned four of their villages and their precious corn crops. This French victory proved decisive for the final outcome of the long conflict against the Iroquois. Hundreds of Mohawks died of starvation during the famine caused by the destruction of their crops, while the Ottawas gradually took over the fur trade from the Iroquois nations. As a consequence of all these negative events, the Iroquois chiefs decided to conclude a peace agreement with the French. After long and difficult negotiations, a definitive peace treaty was finally signed in July 1667. A new era of peace and prosperity for New France had just begun. In the 1660s, in addition to the areas around the St Lawrence River and Acadia, the French had also started colonization of Newfoundland. Around the middle of the century, both the English and French felt an increasing need to establish permanent naval bases near the Grand Banks of Newfoundland, in order to enable their cod fishermen to stop for provisioning their boats.[21] The harbour of Placentia was already used by the French fishermen for this purpose, so it seemed to King Louis XIV the ideal place to establish a new colony. This was founded in 1660 and provided with a small garrison of twenty-five colonial soldiers two years later. However, the soldiers who made up the garrison revolted and killed the newly appointed governor. For a certain period the settlement was abandoned, until the arrival in 1663 of a new group of settlers. More soldiers arrived in 1667, but the colony on Newfoundland continued to struggle for its survival until the arrival of more troops in 1687 (just twenty-five colonial regulars).

---

20   Ibid., p.68.
21   Ibid., p.78.

'French Regiment Carignan–Salières in Canada 1665–1668', by Harry C. Larter, *MUIA Pl. 85*,
© The Company of Military Historians.

French infantryman, late seventeenth century. Public domain picture from the Vinkhuijzen Collection of military uniforms, part of the New York Public Library digital collections.

The flourishing of Canada

With victory over the Iroquois, the colonists of New France could finally settle down to their tasks without having to fear for their lives almost every day. The forts built along the Richelieu River had secured the frontier after many years of Indian incursions, and were now proving to be excellent starting points for further expeditions into Indian territory. The routes to these western regions, which were rich in fur, now lay open to the French explorers and traders. New Indian nations, such as the Ottawas, Ojibwas and Algonquins, replaced the Iroquois as the leading group for the fur trade. These tribes all became important trading partners and military allies for the French. The population of Canada, however, remained very snall. In order to counter this problem, the king started to encourage the regular soldiers sent from France to remain in the colonies, by providing them with the necessary means to establish themselves.[22] The officers, for example, were offered 'seigneuries': this was something simply unthinkable in France, and thus many officers accepted the offer. These measures also encouraged emigration from France, with more than 2,000 people leaving for Canada. With the improvement in the relationship with the Iroquois and the gradual use of soldiers for implementation of a military colonization, the French authorities were encouraged to reduce the numbers of New France's military garrison. By 1671, only seventy-seven regular soldiers were garrisoned in Canada, leaving the strategic forts on the Richelieu River practically undefended. The Iroquois, observing the gradual military weakening of the French, realized that they could take their revenge on the colonists and started to rearm themselves with modern weapons bought from the English merchants. As the English conquered New Netherland, they began to form close commercial and military ties with the Iroquois. The main objective of the English colonial authorities was to use the Iroquois as a force to hinder French colonial expansion.[23] As a response, in 1681, France lifted the ban on the sale of firearms to the natives and started to arm the Algonquin allied tribes, in view of a new conflict against the Iroquois.

The Iroquois' first move was to attack the western tribes favourable to the French, in order to obtain again complete control over the fur trade. The new French trading posts and Jesuit missions were menaced for a certain period, but the danger of a new Indian conflict was initially contained thanks to the intelligent use of diplomacy. In 1682, however, the Iroquois attacked the Illinois, Miamis and Ottawas; these were all allies of the French and thus asked for their military help. Luckily for them, during the previous years the Canadian colonists had gradually developed an excellent system of militia which enabled the French to organize a good defence against the Iroquois and face the dangers of a new Indian war. In any case, with the renewal of hostilities, the militia of New France desperately needed the support of new regular troops: this materialized in 1683, with the arrival of the first three independent companies of the French Navy, known as '*Compagnies franches de la Marine*'. Unlike the army's units, those of the navy were also employed to serve overseas, thus becoming the first 'real' colonial forces of France. They were to constitute the longest-serving units of

[22] Ibid., p.72.
[23] Ibid., p.100.

French pikeman, first half of the seventeenth century. Public domain picture from the Vinkhuijzen Collection of military uniforms, part of the New York Public Library digital collections.

French arquebusier, first half of the seventeenth century. Public domain picture from the Vinkhuijzen Collection of military uniforms, part of the New York Public Library digital collections.

French regulars in Canada.[24] The navy troops proved to be decisive in the outcome of the new Iroquois conflict and increased the process of military colonization already started in New France. During the 1680s, they increased to some 1,500 officers and soldiers.

The last phase of the Iroquois Wars and the Great Peace of Montreal

In June 1687, in order to bring the Indian conflict to an end, New France's Governor Denonville set out with a well-drilled military force to Fort Frontenac, where he had organized a meeting with fifty Iroquois hereditary chiefs. The latter constituted the entire leadership of the Iroquois nations and had been lulled into meeting the French under a flag of truce.[25] Unfortunately for them, the French had prepared a perfect trap: Denonville seized, chained and shipped all the fifty chiefs to France. He then ravaged the lands of the Seneca tribe, including their capital of Ganondagan. Before returning home, the French expedition travelled down the shore of Lake Ontario and built Fort Denonville at the site where the Niagara River meets Lake Ontario. During the following autumn, the French continued their attacks against the Iroquois with even more intensity. In September, an expedition numbering around 3,000 regulars and militiamen was sent to attack Mohawk territory in a punitive raid. The French proceeded down the Richelieu River and marched through the heart of Iroquois territory; strangely, they met no serious resistance and encountered just a few warriors. As a result, the French were able to burn many villages and destroy a large amount of stored crops. This material damage proved to be terrible for the Iroquois, with hundreds of them dying from starvation during the following winter. These events, together with the capture of their main chiefs and the destruction of the Seneca and Mohawk lands, infuriated the Iroquois.[26] Now they had the firm intention of terrorizing New France with a new series of attacks on a scale never seen before. The French soon became aware of this and Denonville used most of his regulars to garrison and protect the various settlements across the land. The colonial government chose to protect the colonists' homes and families instead of the military fortifications, with the result that forts were abandoned to use their garrisons in other places.[27] Despite these defensive measures, the new offensive of the Iroquois was simply devastating. Several farmsteads were destroyed and whole families of colonists captured or killed. Around 1,500 Iroquois warriors harassed the French defences around Montreal for several months, attacking almost every day.

After these failures, Denonville was substituted by Frontenac, who had already been Governor of New France during a previous period. During King William's War, the French created raiding parties with allied natives to attack the English colonial settlements, while the English used the Iroquois to do the same thing against the French. Throughout the 1690s, the French and their Indian allies continued to raid deep into Iroquois territories. Mohawk

[24] Ibid., p.83.
[25] Pieroni, Piero, *I grandi capi Indiani* (Florence, 1963), p.140.
[26] Johnson, Michael G., *Tribes of the Iroquois Confederacy* (Oxford, 2003).
[27] Pieroni, Piero, *I grandi capi Indiani* (Florence, 1963), p.140.

French arquebusier, first half of the seventeenth century. Public domain picture from the Vinkhuijzen Collection of military uniforms, part of the New York Public Library digital collections.

villages were again destroyed in 1692, while Seneca, Oneida and Onondaga villages were raided shortly after. Because France claimed dominion over the Iroquois nations, the French offensives against the Iroquois lands were not halted by the 1697 Treaty of Ryswick that brought peace between England and France. Exhausted by the French attacks, the Iroquois started to change their traditional mentality. They began to see the English as becoming a greater threat than the French, and thus decided that it was probably better to restore good relationships with the colonists of New France. The English settlers had begun to colonize Pennsylvania in 1681, and their expansion in this territory had gradually encroached on the southern border of the Iroquois territory.[28] At the same time, the French also started to change their usual attitude towards the Iroquois: after nearly fifty years of terrible warfare, it was by now clear to the settlers of New France that it was simply impossible to completely destroy the Iroquois nations. As a result, the French decided that befriending the Iroquois was the easiest way to ensure their monopoly of the northern fur trade and help stop English expansionism.

Having different ambitions but common intentions and fears, the French and Iroquois started preparations to agree a definitive peace treaty. As soon as the English colonial authorities heard of this, they tried to avoid the agreement of a definitive peace in every possible way. The latter would have resulted in the loss of Albany's monopoly of the fur trade with the Iroquois and, without the protection of the Iroquois nations, the northern flank of the English territories would have become open to French attacks. Despite the English opposition, the Great Peace of Montreal between the French and Iroquois was finally signed in 1701. According to the peace treaty, the Iroquois agreed to stop marauding and allow Indian refugees from other tribes to return east from the Great Lakes. As a result of the latter condition, the Shawnee regained control of the Ohio Country and of the lower Allegheny River. The Miami tribe returned to take control of modern Indiana and north-west Ohio, while the Pottawatomie went to Michigan and the Illinois tribe to modern Illinois.[29] With the Dutch removal from North America, the English and French had become equally powerful. The Iroquois came to see that they held the balance of power between the two European powers, and used that position to their benefit during the following decades.[30] The Great Peace of Montreal proved to be durable: it would not be until the 1720s that the Iroquois territories would again be threatened by the European colonial powers. In 1701, the Iroquois also signed a new treaty with the English, known as the Nanfan Treaty, according to which the Iroquois tribes gave the English much of the disputed territory located north of the Ohio River. Although this transfer was not recognised by the French, the Nanfan Treaty enabled the Iroquois to have good relationships with the English colonies for the following two decades.

---

[28] Ibid., p.142.
[29] Ibid., p.145.
[30] Ibid.

Chapter 10

The military organization of New France

When Kirke's expedition anchored at Quebec in 1629, the French colony was only protected by a handful of soldiers in the service of the Company of the One Hundred Associates. The colony's garrison remained very small after the return of Quebec to France. The military situation partly changed only in 1636, when Governor Charles Huault de Montmagny was sent to Canada with reinforcements. De Montmagny was an experienced naval officer and a veteran of various naval campaigns against the Turkish and Arab corsairs. Shortly after his arrival, he understood that the colony's military defences needed to be improved and reorganized. Quebec City soon became animated by a much more martial spirit than during the early period under Champlain. War exercises and training of the garrison's soldiers became much more frequent, and started to be conducted on a regular basis.[1] At the outbreak of the Beaver Wars, however, it soon became clear to the French colonists that the few soldiers in the service of the Company were not enough to face the new military threat constituted by the Iroquois. Various requests for military assistance were sent to Paris, but very few soldiers arrived from France. In August 1642, Governor Montmagny only received a contingent of about forty soldiers as reinforcement. In addition, the Queen of France (Anna of Austria), who was particularly interested in protecting the Canadian Jesuit missions from the Indians, provided 100,000 livres to raise and equip a company of sixty soldiers.[2] This was finally done in the winter of 1643–1644 and the new company was distributed among the various parts of the country. This special detachment sent by the queen was finally absorbed into the regular garrison of New France after 1645, which numbered only about sixty soldiers distributed between the main settlements of Quebec, Montreal and Trois-Rivières. Shortly before the Iroquois offensive against Huronia, the French sent a small group of twelve soldiers to help their Indian allies and garrison the advanced Sainte-Marie mission. During the terrible years in which the guerrilla activities of the Iroquois ravaged the territory of New France, the military defences of the colony remained very poor and ineffective: there was only a tiny garrison and a 'flying camp' of a few regular soldiers and volunteers, the latter being used to face emergencies. In 1651 the 'flying camp' was expanded by raising its numbers to seventy; in 1653, however, it was disbanded for economic reasons.[3] As we have previously seen, recruiting and maintaining soldiers was very expensive for the early commercial companies, with the result that military costs were always on the verge of being cut.

---

[1] Chartrand, René, *Canadian Military Heritage (Volume 1, 1000–1754)* (Montreal, 1993), p.52.
[2] Ibid., p.54.
[3] Ibid., p.57.

After 1652, the permanent garrison of New France should have consisted of fifteen soldiers in Quebec, twenty-four in Trois-Rivières and ten in Montreal; in fact, however, it numbered only thirty-five men in total. Following the peace treaty of 1653, twenty soldiers recruited in France were sent to assist the expedition that founded the new mission of Sainte-Marie in the heart of the Iroquois territory. During the terrible years of Indian war, each able-bodied French colonist became a potential soldier. Due to the very small number of regular soldiers, many of the expeditions sent against the Iroquois had to include a large number of civilian volunteers. Despite this, however, a Canadian militia was not formed, at least for the moment. In 1661, with the revival of the Iroquois raids, the Company of the One Hundred Associates sent 100 soldiers to Canada. During October of the following year, another 100 soldiers arrived in Canada from France, divided into two companies. These forces were still not enough to face the Iroquois in an effective and decisive way, but at least a new factor was now at work: they had been raised and equipped under the supervision of Jean-Baptiste Colbert, Royal Counsellor and Intendent of Finance, who was also in charge of the French navy. The dispatch of these soldiers was not yet a direct involvement of the crown in the defence of Canada, but was more a kind of subsidy granted by the king to the Company of the One Hundred Associates.[4] Something was changing in France, but also in Canada. On 27 January 1663, the first organized corps of Canadian volunteers was formed in Montreal: the 'Militia of the Holy Family of Jesus-Mary-Joseph'. The purpose of this new corps was to help Montreal's regular garrison, especially in guard duties. A total of 139 volunteers enrolled in this militia unit, forming twenty squads of seven men each (six militiamen plus a corporal elected by his men).[5] This militia corps was finally disbanded in 1665, with the arrival of the Carignan-Salières Regiment from France.

The Carignan-Salières Regiment

In 1664, for the first time in French military history, some troops were detached from the royal army to serve in the overseas colonies. In the summer of 1665, an entire regiment numbering 1,000 soldiers in twenty companies was sent to Canada. This was the Carignan-Salières Regiment, which derived its name from Colonel Thomas-François de Savoie, Prince of Carignan. The regiment had been raised in Piedmont during 1644 by the prince; during the following decade, however, the unit's recruiting operations were conducted in France, and thus the regiment gradually lost its Piedmontese character.[6] Following the 1659 Peace Treaty of the Pyrenees signed between France and Spain, the number of French infantry regiments was much reduced. The original Carignan Regiment, instead of being disbanded, was merged with another similar infantry unit, the Salières Regiment. The latter had been formed as early as 1630. A few years after the merger, the new Carignan-Salières Regiment numbered 400 men divided into eight companies. When the king chose the unit for service in

---

[4]   Ibid., p.62.
[5]   Ibid.
[6]   Ibid., p.64.

'French Regiment Carignan-Salières and Governor General's Guard in Canada 1665–1668', by Eugene Leliepvre, *MUIA Pl. 493*, © The Company of Military Historians.

Canada, he decided to increase the strength of the regiment to 1,000 soldiers. For this reason, twelve companies drawn from other infantry regiments were incorporated into the Carignan-Salières Regiment: four from the Lellier Regiment, four from the Chambellé Regiment, three from Poitou Regiment and one from Broglio Regiment.[7] Most of the soldiers from these added companies were veterans of the 1664 campaign in Hungary against the Turks. In April and May 1665, the twenty companies of the Carignan-Salières Regiment were inspected in

---

[7]   Ibid.

France before being sent to Canada: apparently, some of them had even more men than they needed. In addition to the Carignan-Salières Regiment, another 200 regular soldiers were sent to New France in the same year. These were divided into four companies, which had been sent to the French West Indies during the previous year. These companies were attached to the Carignan-Salières Regiment, but not incorporated into it, retaining their identification with the respective original regiments. The arrival of the Carignan-Salières Regiment caused enormous enthusiasm in Canada, with hundreds of local volunteers wishing to serve with the unit against the Iroquois. The soldiers of the regiment soon learned how to live and fight in North America, showing a great degree of adaptability.

After the signing of the 1667 peace with the Iroquois, most of the soldiers from the Carignan-Salières Regiment remained in Canada as military settlers, while officers of the unit were given 'seigneuries' and became the new aristocracy of New France. In June 1688, Colonel de Salières returned to France with two companies to begin new recruitment operations there. The other eighteen companies that remained in France were reduced to just four, numbering seventy-five men each. Two of these companies were to garrison Montreal, while the other two were assigned to Chambly. They constituted New France's main garrison forces until 1670, when they were reinforced by five new companies of fifty men each, dispatched from France. The latter remained affiliated with their original regiment back in France, having a detached company status.[8] In 1671, all nine infantry companies were disbanded, with their officers and soldiers being strongly encouraged to remain in Canada as settlers. As a result, the French military presence in Canada was reduced to just twenty-seven men in Quebec City, ten in Montreal and ten in Trois-Rivières, more or less the same situation which was in place before the decisive arrival of the Carignan-Salières Regiment.

In addition to the few forces listed above, there were also twenty men of the Governor General's Guard and a small garrison of ten soldiers at Fort Frontenac (since 1675). The Governor General's Guard was formed in 1665 to act as personal escort for the Marquis Prouville de Tracy, who had been named Lieutenant-General of French America by King Louis XIV. It was a very small unit numbering just seventeen men, commanded by a captain, a lieutenant and a cornet (a second-lieutenant who carried the company's standard).[9] In keeping with the king's wishes, the soldiers of the Governor General's Guard wore cassocks similar to those used by the Musketeers of his own Royal Guard. When the Marquis de Tracy returned to France in 1667, the new Governor Courcelles was not considered worthy enough to have his own company of guards. In 1672, when Count Frontenac was appointed as Governor of New France, the Governor General's Guard was re-established, this time on a more solid base. During his period of rule, Frontenac used his guards as a sort of personal police, which arrested several of his opponents. As a result of this negative experience, in 1682 the royal government specified that the guard had to be used only as the personal escort of governors.[10] Since 1672, the unit had a total of twenty men, known as carabineers.

---

[8]   Ibid., p.67.
[9]   Ibid., p.75.
[10] Ibid.

French Royal Musketeer, second half of the seventeenth century. Public domain picture from the Vinkhuijzen Collection of military uniforms, part of the New York Public Library digital collections.

On paper these were mounted, but in reality they served on foot. The company had to be paid by the single governors, so it was rarely at full strength (usually only during ceremonial occasions). After re-establishment in 1672, its members wore the colours and personal coat of arms of the governor in office.[11]

With regard to the garrison of Acadia, in 1670 the new governor was sent with a company of fifty soldiers to retake possession of the colony from the English. This company was the 6th of the Carignan-Salières Regiment and, like the other ones serving in the St Lawrence

---

[11] Ibid., p.76.

River Valley, was disbanded in 1671. Its soldiers, however, were given the possibility to remain in Acadia as military settlers. After the Dutch attack of 1672, Acadia remained with no regular troops or militiamen until 1685, when a small garrison of thirty regular colonial soldiers arrived. Unlike in New France, militia units were never formed in Acadia, mainly because of the colonists' good relationships with the local Indians.

The birth of the Canadian militia

Until 1669, French colonists in Canada had not been obliged to serve as soldiers, except in emergency situations. In addition, no permanent military organization existed to mobilize them. A letter from Louis XIV, dated 3 April 1669, changed all this: according to it, all able-bodied male subjects of Canada had to be divided into militia companies, with regard for their proximity. They had to assemble once a month to practise handling of arms. In addition, the king's letter prescribed that all militiamen had to be well armed and always supplied with the necessary powder, lead and fuses.[12] These few lines marked the official birth of the Canadian militia: they set a general organization and mobilization programme that would take many years to be fully implemented. It fell to Governor Frontenac, who succeeded Courcelles in 1672, to carry out the considerable organizational effort required by the royal letter that established the Canadian militia. In organizing the militia, Frontenac drew inspiration from the contemporary French coastguard militia.[13] For example, it seemed natural to him to use parishes as the rallying points for the militiamen. Each parish created its own militia company, with the more populous ones having several companies. The internal structure of the militia companies was the same as the regular ones: in all, there would have been fifty militiamen for each company. All the parishes were attached to one of the three districts into which New France was divided: Quebec, Montreal and Trois-Rivières. Each district had a militia staff consisting of a colonel, a lieutenant-colonel and a major. The district governors commanded their local militia companies, while the Governor General of New France commanded all the militia units in Canada. Only religious orders and 'seigneurs' were exempt from service in the militia, but the latter were almost all officers in either the regular troops or the militia.[14]

When an expedition was organized against the Iroquois, there was no shortage of volunteer militiamen willing to participate, with volunteers coming from Montreal being remembered as the most enthusiastic. Montreal's militia units, in fact, were known as the best, but also as the most insubordinate. Rivalries between the various militia units were quite strong and gradually developed over time. Montreal's militiamen, who were practically in a continuous state of war against the Iroquois, considered Quebec's militiamen as 'sheep'.[15] Until the end of the seventeenth century, the Canadian militiamen departing on expeditions received nothing more than food and a few pieces of equipment: they had to supply everything else

---

[12] Ibid., p.74.
[13] Ibid.
[14] Ibid.
[15] Ibid., p.96.

by themselves (including gun, powder horn and clothing). As a result, the main objective of many militiamen taking part in expeditions was to share in any booty or profits deriving from the raids. The large-scale mobilization undertaken during the last phase of the wars against the Iroquois did not offer much promise of booty or profit. As a result, to maintain a high number of militiamen, Governor Frontenac arranged to provide all the militia units with clothing and equipment. This generally included the following: capot (hood), breechcloth, leggings, blanket, moccasins, hunting knife and two shirts.[16] In general terms, the clothing of the militiamen did not constitute a proper military uniform, but was simply Canadian-style civilian wear with some specific elements of military equipment. Since militiamen were not paid, the Canadian militia system proved to be a relatively economical way of maintaining an effective military force with very little costs. The exact number of militiamen to be mobilized for each expedition was determined by the General Governor, who usually launched a general appeal for volunteers coming from the various militia companies. The militiamen who remained behind in each parish cultivated the lands of those who had left as volunteers.

Voyageurs and specialized militia companies

The Canadian militia also included a certain number of canoeists and transporters who did not take an active part in expeditions, but who were fundamental for performing peculiar and more specific roles. These men manned the canoes laden with all the materials needed for large expeditions, being thus known as '*voyageurs*'. Their tasks were extremely arduous, especially during winter. Weapons, light artillery, powder, tools of various kinds, personal equipment for everyone and sufficient food for hundreds of men had to be transported by canoe, for several months and over immense distances.[17] This type of logistical military service, which might appear secondary, was actually fundamental not only for military operations but also for the progressive expansion of New France. Without the impossible achievements of the *voyageurs*, for whom no river was a natural barrier and no distance was too great, the important voyages of discovery that established French sovereignty over vast areas of the North American continent would not have been possible.[18]

In addition to the numerous militia companies that operated according to the normal parish system, there were also some special units with specific functions. In 1687, for example, a new corps of 120 volunteers commanded by four lieutenants was formed in Montreal, with the precise purpose of ensuring the city's safety in case of enemy attacks. This unit, known as the 'Company of Canadian cadets', was disbanded after just one year in existence. As the Canadian militia system developed, the companies from the most important towns started to take pride in naming themselves 'bourgeois militias'.[19] Despite this different denomination, the military obligations of urban militiamen did not change at all.

---

[16] Ibid.
[17] Ibid., p. 97.
[18] Ibid.
[19] Ibid., p. 99.

French arquebusier, mid-seventeenth century. Public domain picture from the Vinkhuijzen Collection of military uniforms, part of the New York Public Library digital collections.

French arquebusier and officer, first half of the seventeenth century. Public domain picture from the Vinkhuijzen Collection of military uniforms, part of the New York Public Library digital collections.

The *Compagnies franches de la Marine*

In 1674, during the conflict between France and the Netherlands, the Dutch Admiral de Ruyter arrived off the French colony of Martinique with a powerful fleet. The settlement was practically undefended but, incredibly, the Dutch assault was repulsed by the few French defenders. This little-known episode, however, had important consequences on the future development and organization of French naval and colonial military forces. Thanks to it,

Louis XIV realized that France had come extremely close to losing one of its most important colonies due to the lack of a proper colonial garrison. As a response to this situation, which was common to all the French colonial possessions, the Ministry of the Navy soon raised a force of 470 men and eight officers for service in the overseas colonies. These were organized into four companies, each detached from a regular infantry regiment (Chambellé, Orléans, Poitou and Lallier).[20] Since its creation in 1669, the French Ministry of the Navy was responsible for both the home fleet and the naval forces stationed in the various colonies (especially in the Americas). The formation of these first naval units started a process that gradually led to the constitution of the French colonial military forces. In spite of their affiliation to the Ministry of the Navy, these new troops, which became known as *Compagnies franches de la Marine*, were not shipboard marines acting as naval infantry but true colonial military forces.

The use of these Navy companies, initially limited to the French colonies in the Caribbean, was soon also established in Canada as a response to the renewed hostilities against the Iroquois. The first three companies of Navy troops arrived in Canada during November 1683, numbering only 150 soldiers who had been recruited in Rochefort.[21] During the following decades, the *Compagnies franches de la Marine* stationed in Canada continued to increase in number: by the end of the 1680s, they numbered around 1,500 officers and soldiers, organized into thirty-five companies. On 24 May 1689, the number of companies was reduced from thirty-five to twenty-eight, always with fifty men each. On 27 May 1699, each company was reduced from fifty to thirty soldiers. From 1689 to 1749, the French regular garrison of Canada consisted of twenty-eight *Compagnies franches de la Marine*. The assignments of the colonial regulars varied greatly: some were used as garrison troops for the most important settlements (usually four companies at Quebec, six at Montreal and two in Trois-Rivières), while others were sent to the small fortified outposts that guarded the frontiers and the precious supply routes of the fur trade.[22] In 1696, two companies were acting as a garrison in Acadia and three in Newfoundland. Officers from the *Compagnies franches de la Marine* were usually selected to organize and command parties of Canadian militiamen, which usually also included native allies. A company of colonial regulars was usually included in each expedition, in order to provide a dependable and disciplined nucleus.[23]

The soldiers of the *Compagnies franches de la Marine* soon learned the basis of Canadian warfare, moving and fighting over rugged terrain with no difficulties. They became experienced bush fighters and a match for the Indians, who had difficulties in countering these European soldiers who had copied their traditional tactics.[24] During periods of peace, the regulars received additional pay for constructing forts and roads. In New France, the new royal garrisons were increasingly required to recruit troops from the local gentry in order to form strong ties with the Canadian population. Like the Carignan-Salières Regiment

[20] Ibid., p.83.
[21] Ibid., p.84.
[22] Ibid., p.87.
[23] Ibid., p.91.
[24] Windrow, Martin, *Military dress of North America 1665–1970* (New York, 1973), p.18.

'*Compagnies Franches de la Marine* in New France 1718–1730', by Michel Petard, *MUIA Pl. 673-674*, © The Company of Military Historians.

before them, the *Compagnies franches de la Marine* contributed to the military colonization of Canada: demobilized soldiers from their ranks became the main source for new settlers, while officers formed much of the colonial ruling class. As time progressed, an increasing number of young men from the new Canadian gentry started to serve as officers in the Navy troops, which had a considerable impact on the social and military life of New France, with the birth of a sort of Canadian military elite.[25] When the first regular colonial troops arrived in Canada, all their officers were French; by 1720, half of the officers were natives of New France.[26]

---

[25] Chartrand, René, *Canadian Military Heritage (Volume 1, 1000–1754)* (Montreal, 1993), p.86.
[26] Ibid.

Chapter 11

The expansion of the English colonies

D uring the second half of the seventeenth century, the original English colonies in North America were joined by new ones, formed as a result of the colonists' territorial expansion and the conquests made at the expense of other European colonial powers. From their foundation, the new colonies adopted the same kind of military organization (based on the militia system) that was already in use in the existing ones.

New York: Soon after conquest from the Dutch, the settlers living in the colony of New Netherland (renamed New York by the English) were organized into a militia. Orders were issued to form militia companies, in which all able-bodied men over the age of 16 must serve. According to these, each militiaman had to provide for himself a musket, sword, bandolier, priming horn and powder horn.[1] In July 1667, the Governor of New York colony ordered that one-third of the militia companies (those serving in the countryside) had to transform themselves into mounted units. Some months later, by November of the same year, one-third of New York's militia consisted of companies of horse or dragoons.[2] Each mounted militiaman had to provide himself with a horse and the relative equipment. The Militia Act of 1677, after the brief Dutch reconquest, re-established the previous militia organization, with one-third of New York colony's 2,000 militiamen being mounted. Very soon, however, this high number of horse militia became impossible to sustain for the settlers, being gradually reduced. During the early phase of King William's War, the northern area of the colony (around Albany) was seriously menaced by French raiders and their Indian allies. As a result, reinforcements and military supplies were frequently sent from New York to Albany. The militiamen raised in the area of Albany proved to be excellent bush fighters, soon adopting the same tactics as their French and Indian opponents with great success. During the early 1690s, Albany was garrisoned by thirty to forty mobilized and paid militiamen, who served together with the English regulars from the independent companies. In November 1700, the militia of New York mustered a total of 3,182 men, organized in eight county regiments: city and county of New York, city and county of Albany, Suffolk, Queen's, King's, Richmond, West Chester and the combined counties of Ulster and Duchess.[3] In addition to these infantry troops, there were mounted units in New York, Albany, Queen's, King's, Ulster and Duchess. Despite this large establishment, shortly before Queen Anne's War the militia of New York had no

---

[1] Chartrand, René, *Colonial American Troops 1610–1774 (2)* (Oxford, 2002), p.35.
[2] Ibid.
[3] Ibid., p.37.

reserves of weapons and was badly trained.[4] To guard the frontier from enemy raids during the conflict, New York mobilized 150 men as infantrymen and thirty as scouts. In 1709, in view of the planned invasion of Canada, three provincial regiments (the first in the history of colonial America) were raised in New York colony. These, however, were soon disbanded when the expedition was cancelled. Originally part of the Dutch colony of New Netherland, New Jersey became predominantly inhabited by English settlers from 1664. Being under no serious military threat, New Jersey's sole military function during the period examined here was that of supporting the militia of New York.

Carolina: The territories of the future southern colonies of Georgia, North and South Carolina were granted as a single Carolina colony from 1629. English expansion over these southern areas was not very fast, with real colonization only taking place during the 1670s. According to the 1669 Constitution of Carolina, all able-bodied men aged between 17 and 60 had to bear arms and serve in the militia when necessary. The first colonists who arrived in April 1670 were all well armed: their military equipment included 200 flintlock muskets, 200 bandoleers, fifty-eight swords, 200 spearheads for pikes and some artillery pieces.[5] Two militia companies were soon formed, which gradually expanded over the years due to the difficult relationships with the local Indians. By 1685, the military of Carolina included two militia regiments (named 'Northward' and 'Southward'), plus a troop of Governor's Life Guards. Later, an independent militia company was added, comprising Huguenots who had fled from France because of religious persecutions.[6] According to the 1696 Militia Act, companies were to drill at least every two months and regiments were to assemble once a year. When the Spanish and French attacked Charleston in 1706, the local militia of what was to become South Carolina included 1,500 men: two companies from Charleston, seven from the 'Northward' Regiment and one from the 'Southward' Regiment. Apparently, all Carolina's militiamen were very well trained. With no regulars being stationed in the colony, a few of them were usually detached to serve for two weeks in garrisons located at strategic points.[7] In 1704, the so-called 'Patrol Act' ordered that ten men out of each militia company had to serve mounted, in order to patrol their district against enemy raids or slave uprisings. Each of the mounted militiamen had to provide a good horse and was to be armed with two pistols, a carbine and sword.[8] In 1710, Carolina's territory was divided into North and South Carolina: the organization of the latter's militia, numbering 1,500 men, remained basically unchanged. Regarding North Carolina, this was sparsely inhabited when it became an autonomous territory; the first militia law was only passed in 1715, with the result that defence during the first five years of the colony's existence had to rely on volunteer militiamen sent from South Carolina.

---

[4]   Ibid.
[5]   Chartrand, René, *Colonial American Troops 1610–1774 (3)* (Oxford, 2003), p.3.
[6]   Ibid.
[7]   Ibid., p.4.
[8]   Ibid.

'South Carolina armed forces 1670', by Tom Jones, *MUIA Pl. 569*, © The Company of Military Historians.

Pennsylvania: The first English settlers arrived in the territory of Pennsylvania during the late 1660s, organizing a small militia of some sort in 1669. The few able-bodied men of these early settlements later came under New York militia law in 1676, having no independent militia structure. The real colonization of Pennsylvania, however, started only in 1681, when the territory was chartered to William Penn from the Society of Friends, a religious group commonly known in England as the Quakers. These were absolutely pacifists, strongly believing that no man should kill another one for any reason. Being persecuted

'South Carolina Militia 1706', by Tom Jones, *MUIA Pl. 625*, © The Company of Military Historians.

in England for their beliefs, they followed the example of the Puritans and obtained the charter for a territory in North America. The Commonwealth of Pennsylvania was unique among the English colonies in North America: it had no military forces and passed no militia laws. A few of Pennsylvania's settlers were not Quakers and thus bore arms for personal defence, but they were a small minority in the colony. Attempts to raise volunteers during Queen Anne's War failed completely, with the first militia units of Pennsylvania being raised only in 1744.[9]

Delaware: Originally settled by the Swedish, Delaware later became part of New Netherland, as did the rest of New Sweden. Following the English conquest of 1664, Delaware became part of New York colony. During this period, the colonial settlements were quite small and had very few inhabitants. From 1669, some militia companies were organized as part of New York's larger militia. Then in 1682, Delaware was separated from New York and included in Pennsylvania. William Penn allowed the area to have its own legislative assembly, which made it an autonomous colony (at the time known as 'Three Lower Counties' of Pennsylvania). Having different religious beliefs from the Quakers, the Swedish, Dutch and English settlers of Delaware continued to have their independent companies of militia as established since 1669.

---

[9]   Ibid., p.9.

Chapter 12

The Dominion of New England

Following the English Restoration of 1660, King Charles II and his government began a process that was intended to bring all the North American colonies under direct control of the Crown. One of the reasons behind this political move was the high cost of administering individual colonies; another one was the need to regulate trade. Throughout the 1660s, the English Parliament passed a number of new laws intended to regulate the trade of the colonies, which were collectively known as Navigation Acts. As we have already seen, these measures were strongly resisted in the New England colonies, where local merchants had established significant trading networks with other English colonies, but also with other European nations and their colonies. The Puritan settlers of New England had always acted with little or no control from London, and had the firm intention of preserving their economic independence and political autonomy. The Navigation Acts outlawed some of the most common New England trade practices and were potentially destructive for the economy of the colonies. As a result, many merchants turned into smugglers, while those who continued trading in a legal way had to pay heavy additional duties (such as increased shipping costs).

The main objective of King Charles II was to cancel the political autonomy of Massachusetts Bay colony, the richest and most important English colony in the Americas. Its inhabitants considered themselves virtually free from any kind of control or imposition from the king. In addition, during King Philip's War, Massachusetts colony had showed its military potential by defeating a great Indian coalition with no help from England. Considering all these aspects, the king saw the New England colonies as a serious and potential threat to his restoration. He repeatedly sought to change the Massachusetts government, but the colonists were able to resist all attempts at reform. Frustrated by this situation, the king decided to attack Massachusetts colony in a legal way: in 1683, legal proceedings began to vacate the charter of the colony, which was formally annulled in June 1684. According to London, the primary motivation for this act was not to attain efficiency in administration, but to guarantee that the purpose of colonies was to make England richer. England's desire for colonies that produced agricultural staples worked well for the southern colonies like Virginia, which produced tobacco, rice and indigo, but not so well for New England. Due to the geology of the region and lack of a suitable staple, the New Englanders generally engaged in trade and became successful competitors to English merchants. In the years before 1684, the New England settlers started to develop workshops that threatened to deprive England of its lucrative colonial markets for manufactured articles such as textiles, leather goods and ironware. Fearing further future developments, the king and government decided to establish a uniform and all-powerful government over the American northern colonies.

The arrest of Sir Edmund Andros during the 1689 Boston Revolt. Public domain picture obtained from Wikimedia Commons.

Establishment and dissolution

The specific objectives of the new kind of government were to include the regulation of trade, reformation of land title practices, coordination on matters of defence and streamlining of the colonial administration into fewer centres. Officially established in 1686, the Dominion of New England included Massachusetts Bay, Plymouth, New Hampshire, Rhode Island and Connecticut colonies. Charles II chose Colonel Percy Kirke to govern the Dominion, but the king died before the commission was officially approved. With the accession to the throne of King James II, a provisional commission was issued to Massachusetts colony native Joseph Dudley, due to delays in developing the definitive one for Sir Edmund Andros. The latter, who had previously been Governor of New York, arrived in Boston on 20 December 1686 and immediately assumed power. He took a very hard-line position from the outset, with the clear intention of cancelling all the colonists' privileges and establishing a strong presence of the English Church in the New England colonies. As a result of Andros' policies, the powerful religious leaders of Massachusetts started to openly oppose his rule and organize a strong dissent targeted to influence the royal court in London. The Puritan pastors thus decided to send Increase Mather to England, in order to press their case against Andros. After being arrested by the colonial authorities, Mather was finally able to reach England only in April 1688. He and some other Massachusetts agents were well received by King James, who promised that in October the colony's concerns would have been addressed. However, the events of the Glorious Revolution took over: by December, James II had been deposed by William of Orange. The Massachusetts agents then petitioned the new monarch and the Lords of Trade for restoration of the old Massachusetts charter. When news of the Glorious Revolution reached New England, the discontented colonists organized a revolt against Andros. In Boston, the pro-King James governor and his royal soldiers were overwhelmed by the Massachusetts militiamen on 18 April 1689. In order to quieten the mob, some pre-Dominion magistrates and members of Andros' council addressed an open letter to the governor, calling for his surrender. Finally, the governor and a number of his supporters were arrested and imprisoned. With the 1689 Boston revolt, the Dominion of New England had effectively collapsed, as local authorities in each colony arrested dominion representatives and reasserted their earlier power. News of the revolt reached New York by April 26, but the local Governor Nicholson did not take any immediate action. Despite being imprisoned, Andros managed to send a request for help to Nicholson, but the latter was in no condition to send any military expedition against the Massachusetts colonists. At the end of May, the same Nicholson was overthrown by the New York colonists, who were supported by the militia in the so-called Leisler's Rebellion. The experience of a centralized government for the New England colonies had totally failed, after less than three years.

English drummer, early seventeenth century. Public domain picture from the Vinkhuijzen Collection of military uniforms, part of the New York Public Library digital collections.

English officer, early seventeenth century. Public domain picture from the Vinkhuijzen Collection of military uniforms, part of the New York Public Library digital collections.

Chapter 13

King William's War

The so-called King William's War (1688–1697) was the North American theatre of the Nine Years' War, which was also known as the War of the Grand Alliance or the War of the League of Augsburg. Like the European conflicts of the previous decades, this was provoked by the expansionist policy of King Louis XIV. It was the first of six colonial wars that were fought in the Americas between the English and French colonies, seeing the massive involvement of the respective Indian allied tribes. At the end of the seventeenth century, the political and military conditions of the English and French colonies were very different in various aspects. There were more than 154,000 English settlers at the beginning of the hostilities, outnumbering the French by twelve to one (the latter amounted to just 14,000 in 1689). Despite this, the French had a series of advantages over the English: first of all, their settlements were more politically unified than the English ones, which were divided into multiple independent colonies that sometimes had contrasting interests. The English settlements were still involved in the political changes following the Glorious Revolution, which created tensions between the colonists. In addition, the English colonial military forces lacked a unified military leadership, something that the French had. Regarding Indian allies, the English had difficult relationships with the allied Iroquois tribes; the French, in contrast, could rely on the total loyalty of their allied natives of the Wabanaki Confederacy. From a military point of view, the French also had another important advantage: the population of New France contained a high number of adult males with military backgrounds. These were all ex-regular soldiers from the Carignan-Salières Regiment and *Compagnies franches de la Marine*, who now served as militiamen. The Canadian military settlers had much more military experience than the English militiamen; in addition, the French could deploy a larger number of regular colonial units thanks to the presence of the *Compagnies franches de la Marine*. The English did not have a similar contingent of regulars and had to rely almost entirely on the colonial militias.

In general terms, neither England nor France wanted to weaken their military position in Europe to support the North American colonies. As a result, no contingents were sent from Europe and the colonial authorities had to rely only on their existing local forces. In the years before the war, tensions had grown on the borders between English and French possessions. The Iroquois were again at war with New France and its Indian allies, as always for control over the lucrative fur trade. At the urging of New England colonies, the Iroquois interrupted the trade routes between New France and its western allied tribes.[1] In retaliation, the French raided Seneca lands of western New York. This escalation culminated in full-scale

---

[1] Pieroni, Piero, *I grandi capi Indiani* (Florence, 1963), p.150.

Indian war when the English supported the Iroquois in their attack against Lachine. At the same time, similar tensions were occurring on the border between French Acadia and New England. The French considered the Kennebec River in southern Maine as the border of their Acadian possessions, but the English colonists from Massachusetts were expanding their settlements in the area, on territory also claimed by the French. To secure their claims to present-day Maine, the French built three Catholic missions near the three largest native villages of the region: on the Kennebec River, Penobscot River and Saint John River. In addition, the French encouraged the five allied Indian tribes living in the area to form the Wabanaki Confederacy.[2] This was created in order to make the political and military alliance of the natives with New France even stronger, with the clear objective of stopping the expansionism of the New Englanders.

The war in Acadia

Acadia was the most important theatre of operations during King William's War, with fighting in the region starting as early as 1688. The commander of the local French military forces was Baron de Saint-Castin, who also acted as military leader of the Wabanaki Confederation. Serving with the Indians of Acadia for several years, Castin had learned every aspect of their way of life, thus gaining total respect and loyalty from his native allies.[3] He even became chief of one of the Wabanaki tribes, soon being considered as a serious menace by the English colonists who had wanted to settle in Acadia for many years. As a result, in April 1688, Governor Andros' forces plundered Castin's home and village on Penobscot Bay; in August, the English also raided the French settlement of Chedabouctou. Castin and the Wabanaki Confederacy responded quickly, the French officer and his native allies launched a raiding campaign along the southern border of Acadia, with the objective of punishing the English and preventing any further expansion of their settlements in the region. Castin's raids began on 13 August and continued for several months until the spring of 1689, killing many English settlers who lived around the Acadian border. In June 1689, several warriors of the Wabanaki Confederacy raided Dover (in New Hampshire), killing more than twenty colonists and taking several captives who were later sold as slaves.[4] In response to Castin's raids, the English sent a small party of twenty-four men in pursuit of the Indian attacking force. However, the English were forced to turn back after losing a quarter of their men in various minor clashes with the natives. In August, Castin led a new Indian war party that captured and destroyed the English fort at Pemaquid.[5] The fall of this defensive position was a serious loss for the English colonists because it pushed the frontier back to Falmouth.

   To face the emergency caused by the success of Castin's incursions, the English authorities decided to send Benjamin Church and his elite rangers to Acadia. Church and his men

---

[2]   Ibid., p.152.
[3]   Ibid.
[4]   Ibid., p.154.
[5]   Chartrand, René, *The Forts of Colonial North America* (Oxford, 2011).

French officer, first half of the seventeenth century. Public domain picture from the Vinkhuijzen Collection of military uniforms, part of the New York Public Library digital collections.

were the only English forces who could counter Castin and his Indians in an effective way, by using the same hit-and-run tactics.[6] In addition, Church's primary mission was protecting the remaining English settlers in Acadia from Wabanaki raids. During the first expedition into Acadia, on 21 September 1689, Church and the 250 men under his command were able to defend a group of English settlers from enemy attacks in the Battle of Deering Oaks. The English colonists were attempting to establish themselves at Falmouth, but were attacked by the Indians. In the ensuing fight, Church lost twenty-one of his men, but the natives were defeated and had to retreat. After the clash, Church decided to go back to Boston, thus leaving the small group of settlers with no military protection. During the following spring, in May 1690, over 400 Canadian and Wabanaki troops returned to the English settlement at Falmouth. Under the leadership of Castin, they massacred all the English colonists at the Battle of Fort Loyal and destroyed the settlement. When Benjamin Church returned to Falmouth later that summer it was too late: he could only bury the dead colonists. During this second expedition to Acadia, Church had the main objective of reconquering Fort Pejepscot, which had been attacked and occupied by the Wabanaki Indians. After completing his mission successfully, Church went 40 miles upriver to Livermore Falls and attacked a native village in retaliation for the destruction of Falmouth. The action was a success and Church's men were able to free some English captives who were in the Indian camp.[7] While retreating, however, Church's party was pursued by a large group of native warriors who attacked it at Cape Elizabeth. Despite suffering some losses, the English were able to retreat and finally reached Portsmouth (New Hampshire) on 26 September.

While these events took place on the borders of Acadia, in May 1690 the New England colonists had decided to attack Port Royal, the capital of the French colony. The authorities of Massachusetts Bay colony had authorized a military expedition against Acadia as early as December 1689, but the plan became reality only after the terrible losses suffered by the English colonists during the Indian raids of early 1690. The expedition set sail from Boston on 28 April 1690, under command of William Phips: it included five ships and a force of 446 provincial militiamen. The English fleet arrived near Port Royal on 9 May. On the following day, Phips sent an emissary to the French authorities. The military conditions of the French defenders were desperate, the garrison numbering just ninety men and having only nineteen muskets. In addition, the fortifications were in the process of being restored and none of the guns were mounted. As a result, the French agreed to surrender without resistance. Despite verbal agreements, according to which Phips promised to protect personal property of the Acadians, the English militiamen plundered both the fort and town. The reasons behind this action are not clear, but it is highly probable that Phips needed as much plunder as possible in order to pay for the costs of the expedition. After Phips' forces abandoned Port Royal, the French settlement was looted and burned by another English expedition, this time of privateers coming from New York. As a result, Governor Villebon had to move the capital of Acadia from Port Royal to Fort Nashwaak (Port Royal was restored as capital only in 1699).

---

[6]   Zaboly, Gary, *American Colonial Ranger* (Oxford, 2004).
[7]   Pieroni, Piero, *I grandi capi Indiani* (Florence, 1963), p.156.

During the summer of 1691, the Wabanaki Indians launched a new offensive against the English settlements in Maine, but were defeated by the local militiamen on several occasions.[8] In early 1692, however, a strong party of 150 Indian warriors attacked York, killing about 100 of the English settlers and burning down many buildings in what became later known as the 'Candlemas Massacre'.[9] As a response, the English authorities sent Benjamin Church to Acadia for the third time. He raided Penobscot with 450 men and then went on to raid Taconock.[10] In 1693, some New England frigates attacked Port Royal again, burning almost a dozen houses to the ground. On 18 July 1694, the French military commander Claude-Sébastien de Villieu, at the head of 250 Indians, raided the English settlement of Durham in New Hampshire. During this action, known as the 'Oyster River Massacre', the French and native forces killed forty-five settlers and captured another forty-nine. In addition, crops were destroyed and livestock killed, thus causing famine for the few survivors of Durham.

In 1696, the French and Indian forces attacked the English settlement at Pemaquid, which had been re-established in 1692 by Sir William Phips, who had also ordered the construction of Fort William Henry to replace the old fort destroyed by the French in 1689.[11] Fort William Henry was the largest in New England at that time: to build it, Massachusetts Bay colony used a third of its budget. The fortification was constructed with stone and mortar, mounting eighteen cannons and having 6ft-thick walls that rose from 10–20ft above the ground.[12] The building of the structure was conducted under the direction of Captain John March, with the assistance of Benjamin Church.[13] The English authorities planned the creation of Fort William Henry as the only effective response to the French and Indian raids conducted against the northern borders of the New England colonies. The French and Wabanaki, respectively led by D'Iberville and Castin, joined forces at Pentagouet in the summer of 1696, with the objective of assaulting the strategic English fortification. D'Iberville commanded 500 French, while Castin descended by river onto Fort William Henry with another 500 Indian warriors. The united French and Indian forces, together with the three ships under command of D'Iberville, laid siege to the fort on 14 August. The English commander, Captain Chubb, initially refused to surrender, despite the large numerical superiority of the enemy. As a result, violent French and Indian assaults went on until the afternoon of the following day (15 August). At that point, Chubb was forced to surrender, arranging for his men to be escorted to Boston and exchanged for French and Indian prisoners held there.[14] After conquering Fort William Henry, D'Iberville was free to launch a new raiding campaign against the English colony of Newfoundland, attacking various villages and killing or capturing hundreds of settlers in the Avalon Peninsula Campaign. Following the French conquest of Fort William Henry, Church was sent to Acadia for the

---

8   Ibid., p.157.
9   Ibid.
10 Zaboly, Gary, *American Colonial Ranger* (Oxford, 2004).
11 Chartrand, René, *The Forts of Colonial North America* (Oxford, 2011).
12 Ibid.
13 Ibid.
14 Pieroni, Piero, *I grandi capi Indiani* (Florence, 1963), p.158.

French pikeman and arquebusier, first half of the seventeenth century. Public domain picture from the Vinkhuijzen Collection of military uniforms, part of the New York Public Library digital collections.

fourth time to launch retaliatory raids. His rangers attacked Acadian communities on the Isthmus of Chignecto and besieged Fort Nashwaack, which was then the provisional capital of Acadia. Many French inhabitants were killed and their goods were looted; houses were burned and livestock slaughtered. Church's fourth campaign was the last military action to take place in Acadia during King William's War.

Governor Frontenac refusing to surrender Quebec City to the British. Public domain picture obtained from Wikimedia Commons.

Frontenac's strategy and the English response

In 1689, the Iroquois, instigated by the English settlers of New York colony, started again to harass minor French settlements by launching a series of raids. Lachine, a small village located upstream from Montreal, was attacked by them in August. The outcome of the Indian raid was a real shock for the colonists of New France: according to Frontenac, the inhabitants of Lachine were massacred with unparalleled and unprecedented violence.[15] The so-called 'massacre of Lachine', however, acted as a formidable catalyst for the French military response. Back in Canada on his second mandate as Governor General, Frontenac soon started to plan his counteroffensive against the English, with the objective of gaining the initiative in the new military operations that were starting. According to his strategic views, the English had to be punished with a severe blow in their homeland, as quickly as possible.[16] As a result, the Canadians decided to surprise the English colonies with attacks by land and during the winter. Frontenac and his staff ordered a simultaneous attack from three different cities of New France: Quebec, Montreal and Trois-Rivières. Three separate expeditions – composed

---

[15] Ibid., p.160.
[16] Ibid.

of Canadian officers, regular colonial soldiers, volunteer militiamen and Indian allies – were prepared in each of the cities. The Montreal column advanced towards the English village of Schenectady, north of Albany, in January 1690. During a delicate night operation, the French entered the fortifications of the village without being seen by the defenders. Every house in the village was surrounded and attacked: the inhabitants were totally surprised and only a few of them were able to escape from the following massacre. Two months later, in March, it was the turn of the column from Trois-Rivières, which attacked the English fort and village of Salmon River, near Portsmouth in Massachusetts. Both the fortification and all the houses of the village were totally destroyed. The Massachusetts militiamen arrived later to pursue the French raiders, but the latter had prepared a trap for them. While the English militia were crossing a narrow bridge over the Wooster River, the French attacked them by firing from the surrounding bush. As a result of this action, twenty English colonists were killed and the column from Trois-Rivières could retreat without further problems. When the Trois-Rivière expedition returned, it quickly joined forces with the column that had been organized in Quebec. The two combined forces marched to Casco, in Maine, which was the objective of the expedition. As with the other two raids, this third one also proved successful for the French.

The three large raids launched by the French and the military events taking place in Acadia convinced the English colonies that New France had to be destroyed once and for all. The English colonial authorities planned to invade Canada in May 1690, both by land and sea. An army of 1,000 militiamen from the colonies of New York and Connecticut, together with a large number of allied Iroquois warriors, was assembled during the following summer at Lake Champlain. However, this force was decimated by sickness, desertion and quarrels between its components, to the point that it was eventually withdrawn. Only a small contingent of the larger initial force remained in service, being sent to Laprairie (south of Montreal). This small attack, however, was repulsed with no particular difficulties by the Canadian militiamen. While all these events took place, Massachusetts Bay Colony decided to organize its own autonomous attack against New France. An army and fleet were soon raised, with the firm conviction that all the expenses needed to organize the expedition would be paid with the large booty taken from the enemy. The force assembled in Massachusetts to attack Quebec was impressive: thirty-four ships and seven battalions of Massachusetts militiamen (each with 300 or 400 men). The overall commander of these forces was Sir William Phips, who could also rely on an artillery detachment with six field guns and a certain number of native allies (serving mainly as scouts). On 16 October 1690, Phips and his fleet reached Quebec, where Frontenac and the French military forces were waiting for them. The Massachusetts battalions landed in the eastern part of the city and marched in perfect European line, with flags flying and drums beating. Initially they met no serious opposition, but were soon ambushed by the defenders (colonial regulars and Canadian militiamen) who were perfectly prepared for street fighting. The ensuing fight ended in a complete defeat for the Massachusetts militiamen, who retreated to their ships after suffering serious losses and abandoning five of their field guns. On 24 October, after just eight days, the English fleet returned to Boston: the victory of the French and Canadian defenders had been complete.

Due to the financial problems following this failed expedition, the economy of Massachusetts Bay colony was severely damaged for several years As a result of this, the colonists learned that any future ambitious expedition against New France had to be conducted with the military and economic help of the mother country.

In 1691, Major Schuyler was sent by the English to attack Montreal with a force of 300 New York militiamen and Iroquois warriors. On the way to his objective, Schuyler attacked Fort Laprairie again, but once more the English attack ended in failure. Repulsed, the militiamen and Iroquois retreated towards English territory. After the English attack, the French quickly mobilized a force of 700 regular soldiers and militiamen, part of which was sent in pursuit of the English and Indian raiders. In the ensuing battle, the New York militiamen were completely surprised, with sixty-four of them being killed, together with seventeen Iroquois. The Iroquois, who were again at war with the French, mounted some offensives of their own against New France, but these were all repulsed and caused even more serious losses to the Iroquois tribes.[17] After the Iroquois raids of 1692, the French counter-attacked. In January 1693, a French military expedition raided several Mohawk villages located north of Albany. As a result of their defeats, the Iroquois began to feel that their new English allies were not powerful enough to support them against the French.[18] Diffidence towards the English was also due to other factors: for example, the Indian allies of the French were all well provided with powder and muskets, but the Iroquois lacked powder and received very few weapons from the English colonists.[19] In 1696, the French launched their decisive offensive against the Iroquois, under the expert military guidance of Frontenac. An army of more than 2,000 men advanced into the heart of the Onondaga territory, destroying all villages and crops encountered. After the events of 1696, it became clear to the Iroquois that they no longer had any chance of defeating the French and that the military alliance with the English colonies was not profitable for them. They thus concluded a definitive peace with the French in 1701, remaining neutral during Queen Anne's War.

Hudson's Bay theatre and the end of the war

In addition to Acadia, New York and Quebec, King William's War was also fought in the extreme north of Canada. English traders were present in Hudson's Bay from 1668, and the English presence in the area was formally established in 1670 with the creation of the Hudson's Bay Company, which was chartered by the English government and received permission to build up fortified trading posts on the shores of the bay.[20] Since the establishment of these first trading posts, a low-intensity economic war between the English and French had started in Arctic North America. In the years before the war, the Hudson's Bay Company had established trading outposts on James Bay and on the southern reaches of

---

[17] Ibid., p.162.
[18] Chartrand, René, *Canadian Military Heritage (Volume 1, 1000–1754)* (Montreal, 1993), p.105.
[19] Ibid., p.104.
[20] Chartrand, René, *The Forts of Colonial North America* (Oxford, 2011).

'Massachusetts Bay Militia 1670–1690', by David Rickman, *MUIA Pl. 717*, © The Company of Military Historians.

Hudson's Bay. From the beginning, it became clear to the English merchants that these were perfect targets for French raiding parties departing from Montreal. As a result, a militia of some sort was organized with the company's servants for military defence of the outposts.[21]

---

[21]   Chartrand, René, *Colonial American Troops 1610–1774 (3)* (Oxford, 2003), p.19.

'Governor Phips' Quebec Expedition 1690', by Peter Copeland, *MUIA Pl. 812*, © The Company of Military Historians.

In 1686, however, Governor Denonville launched the so-called 'Hudson Bay Expedition' from Montreal. A party of colonial regulars and volunteer militiamen, marching overland, reached the small English forts and captured several of them. During King William's War, more French raids followed, mainly by sea: most of the remaining English outposts – including Moose Factory, York Factory and Fort Albany – were taken by French raiders. The latter were led in their successful expeditions by the experienced D'Iberville. In 1693, the English had created a regular independent company of infantry and a small artillery detachment in

French arquebusier, mid-seventeenth century. Public domain picture from the Vinkhuijzen Collection of military uniforms, part of the New York Public Library digital collections.

French arquebusier, late sixteenth century. Public domain picture from the Vinkhuijzen Collection of military uniforms, part of the New York Public Library digital collections.

order to garrison the forts built on Hudson's Bay.[22] However, this was not enough and by 1694 the French were in total control. York Factory was recaptured by the English in 1695, but in 1697, D'Iberville won the important naval clash known as the Battle of Hudson's Bay and later reoccupied York Factory. King William's War ended in September 1697 with the signing of the Treaty of Ryswick, which brought the colonial borders of North America back to the '*status quo ante bellum*'. The French maintained control over Acadia and the outposts conquered in Hudson's Bay. However, many important political questions remained unsettled. Peace in North America was to last for just five years.

---

[22] Ibid.

Chapter 14

Queen Anne's War

In 1702 a new major conflict, the War of the Spanish Succession, broke out in Europe. This time the military operations also spread to the North American colonies, with the reprisal of hostilities between the English and French colonists, together with their respective Indian allies. This time the conflict saw the involvement of another colonial power, Spain, as the most important military ally of the French. The dimensions of Queen Anne's War were larger than those of King William's War, with military operations being conducted in three different theatres. The first and most important was that of Acadia and the border between New England and New France, where most of the battles of the previous war had been fought. The second theatre of operations was the southern one, which saw the English colonists of Carolina fighting against the Spanish who were settled in Florida. The final and minor theatre was that of Newfoundland, where English and French settlers fought for possession of this strategic territory. Queen Anne's War was the first 'continental' war of North America, because in the years preceding the conflict the European colonial powers had gradually extended their territorial control over large new regions. The English settlements had advanced southwards in the Carolinas, while French explorers had located the mouth of the Mississippi River. There the latter established a small colonial settlement in 1699 at Fort Maurepas: from this base the French started to create trade routes into the interior, as usual by establishing friendly relations with the local Indian tribes. Fort Maurepas was initially garrisoned only by a few marines, detached from the ships of the founding expedition. In 1703, orders were given to raise two companies of colonial regulars (with fifty men each), which were to serve as garrison for the new territory of Mississippi.[1] The Spanish, meanwhile, had strengthened their presence in Florida. Similar to the French, Spanish missionaries had established a network of missions in a bid to convert the indigenous inhabitants of the region. At the time of Queen Anne's War, the Spanish population of Florida was quite small, numbering just 1,500, but there were around 20,000 natives who were mostly friendly towards the Spanish settlers.[2]

The northern theatre

When military confrontation restarted in Acadia, little had changed since the days of King William's War. As in the previous conflict, the French had the decisive support of the Wabanaki Confederacy. The French regular garrison consisted of four *Compagnies franches*

---

[1]   Chartrand, René, *The French soldier in Colonial America* (Ottawa, 1984), p.16.
[2]   Pieroni, Piero, *I grandi capi Indiani* (Florence, 1963), p.170.

British officer, late seventeenth century. Public domain picture from the Vinkhuijzen Collection of military uniforms, part of the New York Public Library digital collections.

British infantryman, late seventeenth century. Public domain picture from the Vinkhuijzen Collection of military uniforms, part of the New York Public Library digital collections.

de la Marine. Both the French and Indians shared the same main objective: preventing the English colonists who lived on the southern borders of Acadia from settling in territories north of the Kennebec River. To achieve this, the French and their native allies employed their usual tactic of launching raids against the northern settlements of New England. In 1703, the French commander De Beaubassin led a few Canadian militiamen and 500 Wabanaki Indians in the so-called 'North-east Coast Campaign'. Several New England settlements, from Wells to Falmouth, were raided, with more than 300 colonists killed or captured. In February 1704, the Frenchman De Rouville led another 250 Wabanaki Indians and fifty Canadian militiamen in a raid on Deerfield, in the province of Massachusetts Bay (the heart of the English colony). The settlement was completely destroyed and several of its inhabitants were massacred with incredible violence. More than 100 colonists were captured and later sold as slaves near Montreal, after a long overland march of hundreds of miles. Unable to counter these raids in an effective way, the English colonial authorities decided to launch an offensive against Acadia. The man who was chosen to lead the English operations in the region was the expert and by now legendary Benjamin Church, together with his rangers. Church's expedition raided Grand Pré, Chignecto and other French settlements in retaliation for the Deerfield massacre. The rangers were apparently very effective in their raids. While Acadia's capital of Port Royal was not attacked by them, Church claimed that after his campaign only five French houses were still standing in the region.

Meanwhile, the French proved to be very active in inciting the allied Indian tribes against the New Englanders. Jesuit missionary Father Sébastien Rale, in particular, became one of the most important figures in this process.[3] With the objective of stopping Indian raids caused by the French, Massachusetts Governor Joseph Dudley put a price on Rale's head. In the winter of 1705, the English sent an expedition with 275 men to seize Rale and sack the Indian village from which he was operating. Warned in time, Rale escaped into the woods. The English militiamen, however, burned the Indian village and Rale's church. Despite this temporary setback, French and Wabanaki raiding activities against northern Massachusetts continued for the rest of 1705. In these operations the Canadians and their Indian allies showed complete tactical superiority over the English: the latter were unable to organize an effective defence because the enemy raids happened so quickly. In addition, English reprisal raids were usually mounted against empty enemy camps and settlements, mainly due to the rapidity of the French and Indians in organizing an effective cover for their retreats. Unable to confront the French in guerrilla warfare, the English planned to launch a conventional military offensive against Port Royal, with the ambition of conquering Acadia in a definitive way.

In May 1707, Governor Dudley organized an expedition against Port Royal, numbering 1,600 men led by John March. These failed to take the fort of Port Royal by siege. A follow-up expedition sent to support March's men in August was also repulsed by the French defenders. Now having the initiative, the French launched a new raid against the Massachusetts town of Haverhill in 1708. French raids continued with more or less the same intensity until

---

[3]   Windrow, Martin, *Military dress of North America 1665–1970* (New York, 1973), p.12.

September 1710, when a strong English military expedition finally conquered Port Royal after a week-long siege. The English force numbered 3,600, under the command of Francis Nicholson, with 600 regular soldiers (detached from the regiments of Colonels Holt, Will, Bar, Shannon and Churchill), plus volunteer militiamen organized into four regiments (two from Massachusetts, one from Connecticut and one from New Hampshire and Rhode Island). The numerical superiority enabled the assaulters to defeat the French garrison with no particular difficulties. French resistance in Acadia continued until the end of the war, but thanks to the conquest of Port Royal the peninsular portion of Acadia remained firmly under English control. Resistance was carried on with guerrilla methods, mainly by the Wabanaki Indians, who launched raids along the Maine frontier and defeated the English at the Battle of Bloody Creek in 1711.[4] Despite this local Indian victory, however, Port Royal and the surrounding areas remained in the hands of the English.

While all these events happened in Acadia, the other sectors of the northern front remained quiet during the early years of the new conflict. Despite many English attempts to involve them in the war, the Iroquois did not infringe the peace treaty agreed with the French in 1701 and remained neutral. In 1709, Francis Nicholson and Samuel Vetch started to plan an ambitious invasion of New France, which was to receive financial and logistic support from the English government. According to this project, the English would attack New France with an overland assault on Montreal via Lake Champlain and a sea-based assault by naval forces against Quebec. When the land expedition (that was made up of three New England militia battalions) reached the southern end of Lake Champlain, the English land forces were informed that the naval support needed for the attack on Quebec had been diverted to another front of the war in Europe. As a result, the whole invasion plan of 1709 was cancelled and the land expedition turned back. After this failure, Nicholson and Vetch went to London to arouse Queen Anne's interest in the North American theatre of war. Apparently, both Queen Anne and the government were impressed and decided to give the necessary military support that led to the conquest of Acadia in 1710. After capturing Port Royal, Nicholson returned to England to gain support for a renewed attempt against Quebec. He received the assistance that he was asking for and the new expedition was finally organized.

Admiral Hovenden Walker sailed from England to Boston with a fleet of fifteen ships of the line and transports, carrying 5,000 regular soldiers. These were from seven English regular infantry regiments, five of which had been taken from Marlborough's forces in Flanders: General Hill's Regiment, Kirk's Regiment, Clayton's Regiment, Kain's Regiment, Seymour's Regiment, Windresse's Regiment and Disney's Regiment. After arriving in Boston in June 1711, Walker's forces were joined by those prepared in Massachusetts for the attack against New France, with two militia regiments, including some elements from New Hampshire and Rhode Island. The invasion force now comprised nine warships of the line, two bomb ketches and sixty other vessels, transporting some 7,500 infantrymen and 4,500 sailors. On paper, the French had no chance of resisting such a massive invasion force. However, when the English fleet sailed for Quebec at the end of August, a number of its ships foundered on the rocky

---

[4]   Pieroni, Piero, *I grandi capi Indiani* (Florence, 1963), p.175.

shores near the mouth of the St Lawrence River. This accident was due to fog while the expedition was entering the Gulf of St Lawrence. More than 700 regular soldiers were lost in the
disaster, and shaken by this terrible event, Walker decided to return home with the rest of his
fleet. While this was happening to Walker's expedition, Nicholson had started a simultaneous land advance against Montreal with an army of 2,300 men (all militiamen from various
English colonies). Similarly to the original plan of 1709, the idea was to attack Montreal by
land and Quebec by sea. When Nicholson reached Lake George, he was informed of Walker's
disaster, and as a result, the English land expedition was also cancelled and ended in failure.
Canada was safe without having fired a single shot.

The southern theatre

By the end of the previous century, it was clear to both English and French colonists that
control of the Mississippi River would play a significant role in the future political and economical development of the North American colonies. From the outset it was the French
who had the most visionary and effective ideas of how to control this immense and strategic
waterway. The great military leader and explorer D'Iberville developed the so-called 'Project
sur la Caroline', which called for the establishment of French control over the Mississippi
by creating strong commercial and political relationships with the local natives. The idea
was to use the allied natives to limit the English colonies to coastal areas of North America.
The French would gain total control over the interior regions and also be masters of the fur
trade in the profitable southern markets. Since 1699, the French had a base at the mouth of
the Mississippi River, where, in 1702, Fort Louis de la Mobile was founded. Meanwhile,
D'Iberville started to conclude pacts of alliance with several Indian tribes (like the Choctaw).[5]
Contact with the English colonists was inevitable, as they were advancing in the same regions.
The French presence at Mobile, on the coast, became intolerable for the English, especially
when neighbouring Spanish Florida became an ally of the French at the outbreak of the
new war. The English already had too many interests in the region and a flourishing trade
network. In January 1702, shortly before the beginning of hostilities, D'Iberville had already
suggested to his Spanish allies to arm the Apalachee Indians of Florida, who were among
the main native allies of the Spanish colonists. Before war officially broke out, the Spanish
organized an expedition that departed from Pensacola with the objective of attacking the
trading centres of inland Carolina. The Spanish-led force was mostly composed of allied
Indians from Florida.[6] The English, informed about the attack, organized a strong defence at
the head of the Flint River and were able to defeat the Spanish and their native allies (500 of
whom were killed or captured).

When formal notification of hostilities arrived, the Governor of Carolina, Moore, organized and led a force in an expedition against Florida. The English advance blockaded the
Spanish colonial fortress of Castillo de San Marcos at St Augustine. The siege lasted from 10

---

5   Ibid., p.178.
6   Ibid., p.180.

November to 30 December 1702, but the Carolina militiamen and English regular soldiers (backed by 300 allied Indians) were not able to sieze the main Spanish defensive position. When a Spanish relief fleet arrived from Havana, the English forces returned to Carolina. In 1704, Moore organized a raiding expedition against the Apalachee and Timucua Indian tribes of Florida, which were both allies of the Spanish colonists. The expedition became known as the 'Apalachee Massacre' and practically wiped out both tribes.[7] In 1706, a combined French and Spanish amphibious force from Havana attacked Charleston in Carolina, but was repulsed by the English defenders. In the following years, English raiding expeditions, including large numbers of Indian allies, continued to be sent against Florida, with major campaigns organized against Pensacola (1707) and Mobile (1709). The last phase of the war in the south became a conflict between Indian tribes: the Creek, Yamasee and Chickasaw (backed by the English) against the Choctaw, Apalachee and Timucua (supported by France and Spain).[8]

Newfoundland and Hudson Bay

As we have previously seen, Newfoundland was strategically important for both the English and French fishermen, who had conflicting interests over its territory for decades. At the time of Queen Anne's War, the English had a settlement based at St John's on Conception Bay, while the base of the French was at Plaisance on the western side of the Avalon Peninsula. Both sides also had a number of smaller permanent or seasonal settlements (the latter being used by fishermen). In total, the English settlers in Newfoundland numbered 2,000, while the French had around 1,000. During King William's War, D'Iberville had attacked and destroyed most of the English communities, helped by the support of a militia company raised from French settlers at Plaisance. However, there was still an English presence in Newfoundland. In August 1702, an English fleet attacked all the minor French settlements, but made no attempts against Plaisance; by that time the local French militia comprised several companies (including 300 Basque fishermen).[9] During the winter of 1705, the French governor of Plaisance retaliated for the enemy attacks of 1702 by leading a combined force of French and allied Indian fighters, who destroyed several minor English settlements. The French expedition also besieged Fort William at St John's, but was repulsed by the defenders. In the following summer, the French and their allies continued to harass the English colonists, causing serious material losses. As a response, the English sent a fleet that destroyed all the French fishing outposts located on the northern coasts of Newfoundland. In 1708, however, a strong combined force of French, Canadian and Indian fighters captured St John's and destroyed all the English fortifications. After this victory, the French abandoned St John's, enabling the English to reoccupy and refortify the location in 1709. Unlike Newfoundland, where fighting was intense and frequent, the Hudson Bay territories were not significantly

---

7   Ibid.
8   Ibid., p.181.
9   Chartrand, René, *Canadian Military Heritage (Volume 1, 1000–1754)* (Montreal, 1993), p.161.

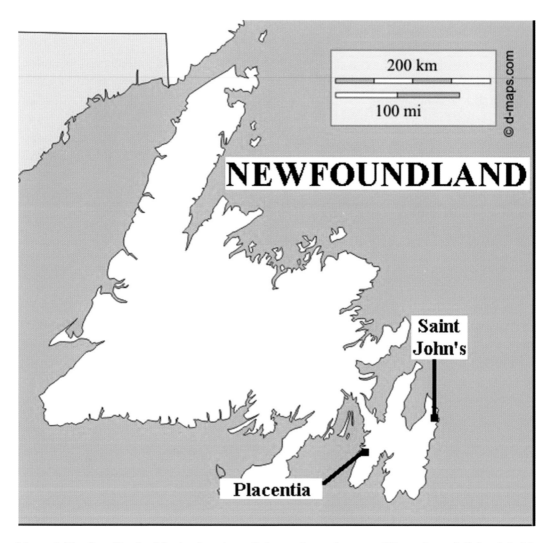

Map of Newfoundland with the location of the main settlements (Placentia and Saint John's). Map modified by Gabriele Esposito; original obtained from http://d-maps.com/carte. php?num_car=23424&lang=en.

involved in Queen Anne's War. The 1697 Treaty of Ryswick left France in control of all but one trading outpost on the bay, Fort Albany. In 1709, the French also tried to conquer this last enemy outpost, but they were repulsed. With the exception of this military action, Hudson Bay saw no military operations until the end of the war.

The aftermath

England and France declared an armistice in 1712, with final peace agreements signed during the following year. Unlike King William's War, the peace that followed the end of Queen Anne's War had very important consequences for the destinies of the North American colonies, marking the beginning of a new era. The territorial changes included in the 1713 Treaty of Utrecht were significant for both the English and French colonies in America. England gained Acadia (which was renamed Nova Scotia), Newfoundland and the Hudson Bay region, most of the territories contested during the war. This might appear strange, considering that most of the military actions in America had been won by the French. However, Louis XIV had been severely defeated in Europe and the highest price for France was paid by the Canadians in North America. According to the peace treaty, France recognized English suzerainty over the Iroquois and agreed that commerce with Indian tribes in the interior of the continent would be open to all nations.[10] Despite the conclusion of hostilities between the two colonial powers, war between the Wabanaki Indians and the English colonists was not over yet. Some native leaders, however, expressed their willingness to negotiate a peace with New England. Governor Dudley organized a peace conference at Portsmouth and peace talks continued later at Casco Bay. The Indians initially wished to maintain the old border of the Kennebec River in order to remain independent from New England. However, with the Treaty of Portsmouth in July 1713, the Wabanaki Confederacy accepted English sovereignty over its territory.

---

[10] Pieroni, Piero, *I grandi capi Indiani* (Florence, 1963), p.185.

Chapter 15

English regular troops in North America

During the early period of their history analysed in this book, the North American English colonies saw little or no deployment of regular troops from the English Army. This was mainly due to two factors: the first was the scarce interest of the crown in its American colonies, whose military needs were considered as secondary compared with those of England itself (involved in European conflicts as well as civil wars); the second was the general love for freedom and autonomy of the American colonists, who always saw the interventions of the central government as a menace to their way of life. For these reasons, very few English troops were sent to the Americas until Queen Anne's War, which marked a decisive change in the military situation of North America. The English colonies were by then menaced by the French in the north and the Spanish in the south, so a presence of European regulars proved to be necessary.

Virginia: To restore order in the royal colony of Virginia following Bacon's rebellion, in October 1676 King Charles II ordered the organizing as soon as possible of a military expedition to be sent to the Americas. At that time the English Army comprised no troops available for service in the colonies, so the authorities had to find a compromise solution in a very short time. On 5 October, just five days after the king's decision, commissions for five companies of infantry (each one taken from existing standing regiments) were signed. These five companies were assembled together in order to form a new regiment of infantry, which was known as Jeffrey's Regiment of Foot from the name of its commander. Each of the five companies had 200 soldiers; in addition, the regiment had a small artillery detachment armed with four 3-pounder guns and two small mortar pieces. Two companies were taken from the 1st Foot Guards, while the other three came from the 2nd Foot Guards, Duke of York's and Holland Regiments. The five companies listed above were supplemented by a further 150 soldiers from non-regimented companies and 500 new recruits raised specifically for the expedition in Virginia.[1] The regimented companies were armed with the then typical musket to pike ratio of two to one, with the exception of the men from the Duke of York's Regiment who were all armed with muskets (their original unit, a naval infantry one, used no pikes).[2] Jeffrey's Regiment received no distinctive uniform, so the soldiers from the five existing companies went to Virginia dressed in the usual uniforms of their old regiments. The recruits and the men from non-regimented companies received a new and unique uniform; regarding

---

[1] Tincey, John, *The British Army 1660–1704* (London, 1994), p.40.
[2] Ibid.

weaponry, they had matchlock and flintlock muskets but no pikes.[3] It is highly probable that the 150 veterans coming from non-regimented companies were all equipped as grenadiers, because 1,500 hand grenades were supplied by the government. An additional 700 muskets and 300 pikes were carried with the expedition, with the intention of using them to equip the loyal units of Virginia militia.

From its formation, Jeffrey's Regiment was intended to be a temporary unit which would be disbanded after crushing the rebellion, with its soldiers returning to their original regiments. When the English soldiers arrived in Virginia, however, the loyal units of the militia had already suppressed the revolt. After some quiet months in America, Jeffrey and his soldiers were ordered to return to England, leaving behind just 100 men (twenty from each of the five companies detached from existing regiments) and any of the regulars who wished to stay as colonists. The 100 soldiers remaining in Virginia were organized into an independent company, and in 1680 these were joined by a second independent company that was raised in England for garrison service in Virginia. The two companies of regulars, however, were badly neglected by the English government, with soldiers becoming mutinous as a result of long delays in their payments.[4] On 7 June 1682, both companies were disbanded, leaving Virginia with no royal troops. During their years of service, the two Virginia companies presumably retained their old uniforms, worn since departure from England. Eight of the English soldiers were retained by the authorities of Virginia to serve as a Governor's Guard; however, it is uncertain how long this small unit remained in service.

Massachusetts: Two independent companies of English regulars landed in Boston during December 1686, with Sir Edmund Andros who had just been appointed by the king as Captain-General and Governor of New England, following the establishment of the Dominion of New England. After the revolt of Boston, the two companies of regulars followed the same destiny as Andros and were sent back to England. In 1709, in view of the planned expedition against New France, three bombardiers were sent from the Tower of London to Boston, with the objective of training the local militiamen in the use of artillery guns. These were later joined by sixty-eight matrosses (gunners' mates) raised in New England[5] for the 1709 expedition against Canada that never materialised.

New York: In September 1664, following the colony's surrender by the Dutch, the first English garrison was established in New York. This consisted of three companies from the Duke of York's Regiment, numbering just 100 soldiers in total. The New York garrison remained the same until the Dutch capture of the colony in 1673. Following the return of New York to England, an independent company of 100 men was formed to replace the three old ones. The original single company was later split into two

3   Ibid.
4   Chartrand, René, *Colonial American Troops 1610–1774 (1)* (Oxford, 2002), p.14.
5   Ibid., p.15.

'Jeffrey's Regiment of Foot 1676–1682', by H. Charles McBarron, *MUIA Pl. 199*, © The Company of Military Historians.

companies of fifty men each in 1686. After being disbanded for a short period, the two independent companies were raised again in 1690, with sixty-eight men and three officers each. In 1694–1695, two more companies of the same kind were added. Reduced to fifty men each in 1699, two years later they were augmented to 100 soldiers each. From 1700, two of the companies were stationed in New York, while the other two were

'British Artillery in Newfoundland 1711–1712', by Barry Thompson, *MUIA Pl. 306*, © The Company of Military Historians.

in Albany. Starting from 1712, the soldiers of the four independent companies were all recruited in America.[6]

Newfoundland: During King William's War, in June 1697, Gibson's Regiment of Foot was sent to St John's in Newfoundland together with a detachment of artillerymen (in total, around 760 men). Hostilities with France, however, were about to end. Most of the force went back to England in September, but a strong garrison of 263 infantrymen and nineteen artillerymen was left behind to protect English interests. In March 1698, the original garrison was greatly reduced, now consisting of just one independent company with fifty-three men, plus seven artillerymen. In 1701, the company was augmented to ninety-nine men in total, plus a detachment of artillery with an officer and six gunners. During Queen Anne's War, in 1705, the infantry company was again reduced to fifty men.

Nova Scotia: Following conquest of Port Royal in 1710, the English had to face almost incessant attacks from the Wabanaki Indians of Acadia. To counter these in a more effective way, the colonial authorities decided to add a corps of rangers to the garrison made up of regular soldiers (comprising four independent companies of infantry of forty men each, plus an artillery detachment). An independent company of rangers was thus formed, with fifty-six Mohawk allied Indians commanded by two English officers. The unit became operative in 1712, when each Mohawk ranger received a blanket and a gun as personal equipment.[7] Camping outside the fort of Port Royal, the rangers served with great success against both Wabanaki raiders and English deserters from the garrison. After a year, however, many Indians deserted and went back to their home villages. As a result, in May 1713 the remains of the unit went to Boston, where it was finally disbanded.

---

[6]   Ibid., p.13.
[7]   Chartrand, René, *Canadian Military Heritage (Volume 1, 1000–1754)* (Montreal, 1993), p.166.

Appendix I

Warfare and tactics in colonial America

In general terms, warfare in colonial America was always governed by three main factors, especially during the period examined in this book: geographical isolation, political changes happening in the mother countries and the independent nature of most of the colonists.[1] In the period 1607–1713, all the European powers that colonized North America were almost always involved in large conflicts between themselves, mainly fought for predominance in Europe. Wars and peace treaties followed one another in quick succession, and very few of the conflicts proved to be decisive in shaping the destinies of the warring states. This political and military situation was reflected in the American colonies, which were initially not particularly involved in the wars of their mother countries. However, as the American settlements became larger and more profitable, there were conflicting commercial interests for the colonial powers. With the general decrease of the Indians' number, new borders between European possessions came into being, with the result that two powers which did not share a land border in Europe now had a long common frontier in the Americas. Colonialism in North America and other parts of the world was gradually transforming European conflicts into global ones, a process that would be completed around the middle of the eighteenth century. Geographical isolation, however, had a strong influence over the political relations between the mother countries and the American colonies: sometimes notice of wars ending in Europe did not reach the American settlements for several months, during which the colonists continued to fight for no purpose. In addition, while European wars were dominated by the traditional laws and codes of diplomacy, the American conflicts had no formality to respect: no official declarations of war were needed to launch raids and stable peace treaties were rarely agreed. War was continuous and had no rules: it was a condition of the soul, a basic component of the colonial way of life. As a result of this, the European settlers had to change their traditional mentality and adopt that of the Indians. Even during times of peace in Europe, the American colonies were always encouraged by their respective mother countries to deliver pin-prick raids on one another. America was the land of wars not officially declared, the arena where the European powers could show their military potential to their rivals or send political messages about the situation in Europe. As a result of this practice, the colonists were often 'used' by the central governments, with no advantage for their own settlements.

In addition to all this, there were the Indians. Unpredictable and sometimes primitive, they were scattered across an inhospitable wilderness in hundreds of tribes.[2] If the colonists

---

[1] Windrow, Martin, *Military dress of North America 1665–1970* (New York, 1973), p.8.
[2] Ibid., p.9.

French arquebusier and standard-bearer, early seventeenth century. Public domain picture from the Vinkhuijzen Collection of military uniforms, part of the New York Public Library digital collections.

were used by their mother countries, the Indians were used by the European settlers. When the Europeans arrived in the Americas, they found no large or unified states, but a multitude of groups who were constantly at war against each other. This political situation was perfect for the colonists, who used remarkably well the traditional divisions between the Indians in order to form military alliances with them and cause new and more destructive inter-tribal wars. As time progressed, each Indian tribe chose a European ally for which to fight, with the result that old tribal rivalries were substituted by new ones for the monopoly of trade with the Europeans. Receiving new weapons from the colonists, the Indians also changed their style of warfare, which became much more violent and led to an increase in the loss of life. But the Europeans also contributed to the destruction of the natives in other ways, for example by introducing new epidemics and diseases into America which killed many thousands of Indians.

Warfare in colonial America, especially during the early years, was absolutely heroic: the settlers, before facing their enemies on the field of battle, had to survive in a totally hostile natural environment. The first and main objective of every community was surviving the local conditions. Being only sporadically supplied by the mother countries, which initially had very little interest in the development of the American colonies, the settlers were obliged to improvise every necessity from the few materials that were locally available.[3] The few expeditions coming from Europe arrived in small numbers, at great cost and after long delays. As a result of this situation, the efforts required to maintain any military force under arms were enormously greater than in Europe. The size of the colonial forces were thus always very small compared with those of contemporary European armies. Minor clashes, which would have been negligible patrol actions in Europe, assumed in the Americas the importance of great and decisive battles.[4] Just moving across the vast expanses of North America was a great risk for any military expedition, and the environment could often be a more terrible enemy than the Indians or other European colonists. As we have seen, regular soldiers from the mother countries were very rarely sent to the Americas. Until Queen Anne's War, they were usually despatched only to quell internal rebellions of the colonies. During most of the period under examination, the only organized military force in the Americas was the colonial militia.

In the North American colonies, all the able-bodied males aged between 16 and 60, be they freemen or servants, were compelled to be enlisted into their local militia and attend musters and training days. The latter occasions were considered serious events in the American colonies, at least during the period analysed in this book, as in the early years of colonization, the survival of a community and its settlement depended mainly on the efficiency of its militia forces.[5] The frequency of training varied a lot, from time to time and colony to colony. At the beginning of the seventeenth century, militiamen of Massachusetts and Virginia trained once a week; some decades later, training only took place on a few days throughout the year (generally, musters were made once per year). Frequency and efficiency of training tended to be

---

[3] Ibid., p.10.
[4] Ibid.
[5] Ibid.

considerable in frontier communities exposed to enemy attacks, becoming less so as the colonial frontiers advanced and the immediate threats receded westwards.[6] As time progressed, some social categories started to be exempted from service in the militia: these included magistrates, public notaries, deputies to a legislature, ministers of the church, schoolmasters, students, physicians, masters of ships, fishermen and herdsmen. All militiamen were required to present themselves at training days properly armed and equipped. In addition, they had to respond to the calls of colonial governors in case of emergency. In times of relative peace, the activities of the militia were conducted on a local basis and for limited periods of time.

Until the last quarter of the seventeenth century, the English colonies did not cooperate in an efficient way from a military point of view. Each emergency was usually faced using a very local mentality, partly because the expenses for expeditions had to be paid entirely by the single colonial communities. The situation changed only during King Philip's War, thanks to which the English settlers (at least those of New England) understood that the new menaces which were emerging needed a more joint response. Professionalism and military preparation became increasingly important. In the early days of the colonial militia, military commanders usually came from local prominent families, being chosen by popular vote and not for their military skills. They had various administrative obligations besides bearing arms: senior officers, for example, usually had to pay for their company's drums and colours.[7] No officer was paid, but serving in the colonial militia was a great honour for each influential man living in the American colonies. This personal prestige had a series of positive consequences for the social life of each militia officer. Senior officers were usually appointed by the colonial legislature, while junior ones tended to be chosen by their men through elections. With the progress of time this situation gradually changed, resulting in the birth of a new and much more professional class of colonial officers.

The early militia units were organized along very similar lines to the contemporary English 'Trained Bands', with proportions of musketeers and pikemen. Each company numbered about fifty men, coming from the same village or town ward, and could be part of a larger county militia regiment. Regarding cavalry and artillery, troops of mounted militiamen appeared only in the 1640s, while artillerymen were usually individual specialists rather than gunners grouped into separate units.[8] Militia laws generally contained many precise obligations regarding the weaponry and equipment that each militiaman had to carry. If men did not meet these requirements, they were usually fined and their money was used to buy flags and drums for the company.[9] By the mid-seventeenth century, pikes became quite rare, as was any kind of personal armour, while heavy matchlock muskets with rests, very popular in the first decades of the century, were gradually replaced by lighter flintlock snaphance muskets. By the 1640s, colonial militiamen were almost all armed with flintlock muskets, in addition to which they usually carried swords, hatchets or cutlasses as secondary weapons. Cutlasses,

[6]   Ibid.
[7]   Chartrand, René, *Colonial American Troops 1610–1774 (1)* (Oxford, 2002), p.23.
[8]   Ibid., p.24.
[9]   Ibid.

French pikeman, first half of the seventeenth century. Public domain picture from the Vinkhuijzen Collection of military uniforms, part of the New York Public Library digital collections.

in particular, were very popular because they were relatively short, heavy and broad-bladed. Swords became less popular during the later decades of the seventeenth century (being omitted from militia laws), while bayonets arrived in the Americas only with the issue of government muskets during the eighteenth century. In the early decades, halberds for sergeants were quite common, while half-pikes and gorgets for officers were generally rare. Some simple uniforms only started to be used around the end of the seventeenth century, but even then on a very limited scale.

When the first soldier-colonists arrived in North America at the beginning of the seventeenth century, they were still equipped with helmets and armour, being ready to use the same basic military tactics that they had learned in Europe. After a few years, however, they soon learned that the only way to fight and survive in the Americas was to adopt the same tactics and kind of warfare employed by the natives. The enormous distances and natural environment of North America required the development of a totally new kind of warfare, mixing Indian tactics with modern European weapons. From the earliest days of colonization, the French handled their relationships with the Indians with more subtlety and skill than the English: as a result, they copied and adopted Indian tactics before and better than the other European settlers. French Jesuit missionaries acted both as intelligence officers and guerrilla leaders, providing the Indians with large amounts of brandy and muskets.[10] Living and fighting with the natives, the Canadians became better than their teachers in conducting warfare with North American tactics. As a result, the barbarous standards of Indian warfare came to be widely accepted as normal in colonial America.

Close-order pitched battles were obviously out of the question, for many reasons. The wooded hills of North America ruled out rigid European-style manoeuvres and made any use of cavalry practically impossible. In the American colonies there were never enough men to assemble massed infantry regiments or battalions like in Europe, the independent spirit of most of the colonists also usually resisting European regimentation and authority.[11] The high level of discipline required to conduct seventeenth and eighteenth-century military manoeuvres was impossible to achieve in the Americas. The Europeans initially had great difficulties in launching offensive operations against the Indians. In defence they could use their much more modern weapons and skills in constructing fortifications, but launching attacks against the Indians in the woods was something totally different. In the forests, the natives were unbeatable: their whole traditional culture, based on hunting, forged them for a war of silent stalking and ambush.[12] The first Europeans who adapted to the Indian war skills were the solitary trappers and hunters, who lived a harsh life along the borders of the colonies. They soon learned how to live and fight in the great North American forests, becoming no less crafty and ruthless than the Indians.[13] In times of war, hunters and trappers transformed themselves into perfect raiders and guides for the parties of militiamen, having much more experience of

---

[10]   Windrow, Martin, *Military dress of North America 1665–1970* (New York, 1973), p.12.
[11]   Ibid.
[12]   Ibid.
[13]   Ibid., p.13.

French pikeman and arquebusier, early seventeenth century. Public domain picture from the Vinkhuijzen Collection of military uniforms, part of the New York Public Library digital collections.

fighting in the woods than the average settlers. As time progressed, these men became known as *Coureurs de Bois* in New France and rangers in New England.

After considering all the elements briefly explained in this Appendix, it is not difficult to understand why the thousands of American militiamen who mustered for war against Britain in 1775 were so effective in fighting European regulars. The American militia system had already been in existence for more than a century, and was perfectly efficient. Every American was a militiaman and had a certain degree of familiarity with weapons and military organization, thanks to which the patriots of 1775 soon assembled a strong military force to oppose the British Army, clearly showing their superiority in the use of North American tactics.[14] Unlike the European soldiers, almost all the American militiamen were potential rangers, who could fight incredibly well in the natural environment surrounding them. Their capacity to mobilize, defend territory and fight for freedom was without doubt inherited from the colonial militias that had existed since 1607.

---

[14] Chartrand, René, *Colonial American Troops 1610–1774 (3)* (Oxford, 2003), p.39.

Appendix II

Plate commentaries and uniformology of colonial America

Plate A: The early colonial militias

Figure 1: Sergeant, Massachusetts Militia, 1636

During the early decades of colonization, both the Massachusetts and Virginia militiamen were usually quite well equipped. Unlike the Virginia colonists, who preferred using lighter quilted armour, those of Massachusetts and the other New England colonies preferred wearing breast and back plates of traditional armour, as shown here. The helmet is a morion, which was very popular, especially among pikemen; as is clear from the use of the halberd, our man is a sergeant. In addition to the normal militia companies, in 1635 the General Court of Massachusetts ordered the creation of a special Governor's Guard, consisting of just six sergeants armed with halberds and swords. These men served during the ceremonial first day of the legislature's session, their number being reduced to two thereafter.[1] The general appearance of this small ceremonial unit must have been more or less the same as our figure. The Military Company of Massachusetts, formed in 1638, was dressed very similarly to the London Artillery Garden, after which it was patterned. Many of the Boston unit's initial members had already served in the London Company, so it is highly probable that they retained their old dress: buff leather coat worn over a red cloth coat, red breeches and red plume on the helmet.[2]

Figure 2: Militiaman, Connecticut Militia, 1637

During the Pequot War, Connecticut militiamen were usually very well equipped with corselets and helmets. The latter, in particular, could be of various kinds: our man is wearing a simple cabasset, but morions and burgonets were also very popular. Contemporary militiamen of Virginia would have probably preferred brigandines or jacks, or even lighter buff coats: the latter were usually worn under corselets for further protection. As time progressed, around the end of the 1640s, traditional armour gradually went out of use, while buff coats remained popular until the last decades of the century. The same happened with helmets and pikes, which were of no practical use by the 1660s/1670s. In the early decades of colonization, some senior and rich officers would even wear heavy three-quarter armour. However, they soon learned how impractical this was for use in North America.

---

[1]   Chartrand, René, *Colonial American Troops 1610–1774 (2)* (Oxford, 2002), p.42.
[2]   Ibid.

Plate B: The Virginia Militia in Bacon's Rebellion

Figure 1: Militiaman, Virginia Militia, 1676

By the time of Bacon's Rebellion, the militiamen of Virginia were equipped in a very simple way, with no armour or helmets. Matchlock muskets were still in use, but were gradually being replaced by the more modern and lighter flintlock muskets. Our militiaman is armed with a flintlock, but still carries the so-called '12 Apostles'. These cartridges were made of wood and carried measured powder charges, were attached to a leather bandolier and could be more than the usual twelve. The basic equipment of a musketeer, as shown in various figures of our plates, also included a powder flask and a small leather bag: the former contained the finer powder used to prime the musket, while the latter was used to carry musket balls. During Bacon's Rebellion, part of the militiamen sided with the rebels. Since there were no uniforms, the rebel forces were practically indistinguishable from those loyal to the governor.

Figure 2: Trooper, Virginia Militia, 1676

From the 1640s, the American colonies of the south deployed a certain number of mounted militiamen, organized in small cavalry troops and commonly known as rangers. They were not real cavalry, but units of mounted light infantry that had the function of guarding the frontiers of the colonies (as a sort of mounted police). In doing this, they were frequently responsible for the defence of some fortifications (small forts or outposts). Due to the basic features of the colonial natural environment, American cavalry was from the beginning very light: the troops of rangers described above were equipped exactly like foot militiamen and wore no armour or helmets. Some militia cavalry, however, were sometimes equipped with buff coats and corselets, as in our case; this was particularly true for mounted officers. In the northern colonies such as Massachusetts, by contrast, some troops of cavalry were heavily equipped in the European manner. During the 1670s and 1680s, mounted militiamen of Massachusetts Bay colony were equipped exactly like the Ironsides of Cromwell, with triple-barred lobster-tail helmet, corselet, buff coat, sword, carbine and pistols. Both the helmet and corselet were painted in black to protect them from rust.[3]

---

[3] Ibid., p.43.

Plate C: Colonial militias in the late seventeenth century

Figure 1: Trooper, Albany Troop of Horse, New York Militia, 1687

The one shown here is probably the first real 'uniform' ever worn by the militias of the North American colonies. The Albany Troop of Horse was formed in March 1685, as part of the New York Militia. According to contemporary reports, the two officers and thirty-six troopers of this small unit were all dressed in dark blue duffel coats.[4] Since no secondary colours are mentioned, it is reasonable to suppose that this very simple uniform was entirely dark blue. The rest of the equipment, including riding boots, was the standard one for the cavalry of those years. In 1693, the unit changed its denomination and was transformed into a troop of dragoons. In the last years of the seventeenth century, various colonial troops of cavalry or dragoons started to receive simple uniforms like the one represented here. The Somerset County Dragoons, for example, were a mounted unit from the Maryland Militia that received arms and equipment from England in 1695, and probably had red duffel coats as a basic uniform.[5]

Figure 2: Ranger, Benjamin Church's company, Plymouth Militia, 1676

During King Philip's War, many companies of militiamen from Massachusetts, Plymouth, Connecticut and Rhode Island took part in military operations in the woods against the Indians. These militiamen acquired many new skills thanks to their participation in these kind of operations, soon adapting to a rapid kind of warfare that was conducted in woods and swamps. The best at doing this were Benjamin Church's rangers, the best fighting men available at the time in New England. The rangers had no distinctive uniform, but were dressed like all the other militiamen in their everyday clothes. Buff coats like that shown here, with or without sleeves, were very popular for protection against enemy arrows. Church recommended his men to wear moccasins and have hatchets as secondary weapons for close fighting: our ranger has normal shoes, but carries a hatchet slung in an old sword baldric. On the field, colonial militiamen usually did not have bandoliers, because of the rattling noise made by the wooden '12 Apostles'.[6]

---

[4] Ibid.
[5] Ibid.
[6] Ibid., p.42.

Plate D: English regular soldiers in the Americas

Figure 1: Grenadier, Jeffrey's Regiment, Virginia, 1677

Unlike the five companies detached from existing regiments, the recruits and men from non-regimented companies who were added to Jeffrey's Regiment received the new and peculiar uniform shown here. This consisted of red coat with light blue cuffs, light blue waistcoat and breeches. As clear from the brown fur cap, our soldier is a grenadier;

musketeers had black hats trimmed with white lace. For grenadiers only, both the front of the coat and the cuffs had additional medium blue lacing. The 650 recruits and soldiers from non-regimented companies were armed only with matchlock and flintlock muskets, having no pikes; 500 hatchets were also issued. Judging from the number of hand grenades given to them, it is highly probable that the 150 veterans from non-regimented companies were all equipped as grenadiers. The five companies detached from existing infantry regiments continued to carry their uniforms: the two companies from the 1st Foot Guards wore red coats with blue facings; the company from the 2nd Foot Guards wore red coats with green facings; the company from the Holland Regiment wore red coats with cream facings; and the Duke of York's Regiment wore gold coats with red facings. The soldiers of the two independent companies that remained in Virginia after the end of the rebellion presumably retained their old uniforms.

Figure 2: Musketeer, Duke of York's Regiment, Virginia, 1678

The Duke of York's Regiment, also known as Admiral's Regiment, was formed on 28 October 1664 with an initial strength of 1,200 men (divided into six companies with 200 soldiers each), who were recruited from the Trained Bands of London as part of the mobilization for the Second Anglo-Dutch War. The unit derived its name from the Duke of York and Albany, Lord High Admiral and brother of King Charles II. In many respects, this regiment can be considered the first ancestor of the Royal Marines, being the first unit of naval infantry ever formed in England. From its formation, the Duke of York's Regiment had a very important role in the military history of colonial America: three of its companies were detached to form the military garrison of New York after capture of the colony from the Dutch in 1664, while one of its companies was detached to form Jeffrey's Regiment in 1676. The peculiar gold and red uniform reproduced the livery of the Duke of York and Albany. All the soldiers of this unit were armed with flintlock muskets, because matchlock ones were impractical for the duties performed on ships by these naval infantrymen. Obviously they had no pikes. The white waist sash shown in our plate was issued to new recruits from 1678 in order to make them recognizable.

Regarding the uniforms of the other English regulars sent to the Americas during the period covered in this book, here are some basic details. The independent companies sent to Massachusetts, New York, Newfoundland and Nova Scotia were all dressed with the royal livery, having red coats lined with blue, red breeches and black hats trimmed with white lace. This same kind of dress was also issued to the New England militia units raised for the 1710 expedition against Acadia and the 1711 expedition against Quebec. Gibson's Regiment, which was sent for a brief period to Newfoundland, was dressed similarly to the independent companies, but with yellow as facing colour instead of blue. Regarding the artillery detachments, which were sent to Massachusetts, Newfoundland and Nova Scotia, they wore the same uniform that was provided by the Board of Ordnance of the Royal Artillery to the artillerymen serving in Europe. This consisted of red coats lined with blue, blue breeches and black hats trimmed with yellow lace. The front of the coat, the cuffs and pockets had additional yellow lacing.

Plate E: New Netherland and New Sweden

Figure 1: Musketeer, New Sweden's garrison, 1654

The few soldiers who made up the military garrison of New Sweden were armed and equipped exactly as any other European soldier of the time. The Swedish Army, under the guidance of the great Gustavus Adolphus, was the first in Europe to adopt some early kind of uniform, but from the sources we have, it seems that no particular dress was ever issued to the soldiers sent to garrisons in the Americas. Regarding weaponry, the soldiers of New Sweden had older weapons than their Dutch opponents: in 1654 they were still armed with matchlock muskets, though a plan to convert them to flintlocks had already been made.[7] This musketeer wears the typical Swedish hat of the time; pikemen probably preferred using helmets, as suggested by some archaeological finds.

Figure 2: Sergeant, Corps of Marines, New Netherland, 1673

The Dutch Corps of Marines has an early history which is very similar to that of the Royal Marines. Like the Duke of York's Maritime Regiment, it was formed on 10 December 1665 as part of the mobilization for the Second Anglo-Dutch War. Its founders were the Prime Minister of the Dutch Republic, Johan de Witte, and the great Admiral Michiel de Ruyter. In 1673, the colony of New Netherland was reconquered by 600 marines, a strong detachment of whom remained to garrison in America until the territory of New York was returned to England. The Dutch Marines initially had no distinctive uniform and were dressed like all the other infantry units, but with the omission of the steel cuirasses then generally worn.[8] In 1672, however, they were issued with the elegant uniform shown here: brown beaver hat with no decorations, blue collarless coat with yellow cuffs and pewter buttons. The colour of the breeches varied, with red, brown and grey all being used. Stockings could be blue or grey. Soldiers and NCOs wore the white shirt collar outside the coat, in place of the neck-cloth worn by officers. Both officers and sergeants had an orange sash around the waist, to distinguish themselves. In addition, officers wore a gorget while sergeants and corporals had a bunch of white ribbons on the right shoulder.[9] Each Dutch marine was armed with flintlock or snaphance musket and sword, the muskets having plug bayonets. Equipment included one crossbelt for the sword and another for the leather pouch (containing bullets and other things), plus a powder flask.

The other soldiers of New Netherland, regulars or militiamen, were armed with match-lock or flintlock muskets, swords and cutlasses. During the early years of the colony, buff coats and helmets were very popular for protection against Indian arrows. Apparently, mail shirts also continued to be used well into the 1640s: in 1641, for example, a request was made for 200 coats of mail to be sent to New Amsterdam.[10] By the middle of the following decade, however, mail shirts were no longer in use.

---

[7]   Chartrand, René, *Colonial American Troops 1610–1774 (1)* (Oxford, 2002), p.43.
[8]   Windrow, Martin, *Military dress of North America 1665–1970* (New York, 1973), p.15.
[9]   Ibid.
[10] Chartrand, René, *Colonial American Troops 1610–1774 (1)* (Oxford, 2002), p.43.

Plate F: The soldiers of New France

Figure 1: Officer, Carignan-Salières Regiment, 1665

The Carignan-Salières Regiment was one of the first French infantry regiments to be dressed in uniform, as part of a process launched by King Louis XIV in the early 1660s. At the time when the unit was sent to Canada, French dress regulations required only that soldiers had to be well clothed and shod, without indicating any further detail about uniforms.[11] Generally speaking, each colonel was responsible for the appearance of his own regiment and thus could dress it as he preferred. The Carignan-Salières was an exception to this rule, because when its soldiers arrived to Canada they all wore a distinctive dress. This included a wide-brimmed black felt hat, similar to that worn by contemporary French peasants; the brim was turned up at the front and sometimes also at the back. They had a long and collarless dark brown frieze coat, lined with grey coarse cloth. The sleeves ended about mid-forearm, turning back into broad grey cuffs. Brown cloth-covered buttons ran the full length of the coat, while the buttons of the cuffs were covered in grey. Pocket flaps were set low on the hip on each side. They also wore a grey waistcoat, dark brown breeches and stockings.[12] The only decorations of this sober and practical dress were some loops of buff and black ribbons gathered on the point of the shoulders, at the end of the garters, on the black leather shoes and at each end of the hat. Drummers, like in all French infantry regiments, were dressed in coats bearing the colours of the colonel's livery: those of the Carignan-Salières Regiment wore a red coat lined with blue, decorated with white and blue livery lace. No official dress regulations existed for officers, but those serving in the Carignan-Salières Regiment were usually dressed quite similarly to their men. The only differences represented in our figure are the grey hat (instead of the usual black one) and the white sword-belt decorated with violet silk fringes. During their first winter in Canada, the soldiers of the Carignan-Salières Regiment quickly adopted some elements of the local winter dress, such as hooded overcoats, mittens, moccasins, tuques and leggings. All the soldiers of the Carignan-Salières Regiment were armed with matchlock or flintlock muskets: apparently, the pikes of the regiment were left in France, being replaced by the plug bayonets of the muskets.[13] At that time flintlock muskets were forbidden in France, but the Carignan-Salières Regiment had 200 of these. Each soldier also had a short sword.

Figure 2: Musketeer, Governor General's Guard, 1665
The Governor General's Guard was formed in 1665 to act as a personal escort for the Marquis Prouville de Tracy, the Lieutenant-General of French America. During the first years of its existence, this small company-sized ceremonial unit was dressed exactly like the Royal Musketeers of Louis XIV, by royal permission due to the personal prestige of the Marquis Prouville de Tracy. The uniform consisted of a black hat with red band and white plume, and blue cassock lined with red and edged with silver lace. This bore on the front, back and side panels a badge consisting of a white cross with fleurs-de-lys at the end of its arms and a red sunburst at its centre. The clothing worn under the cassock was blue, while breeches were white and stockings were red. White leather gloves completed the outfit. The weapon is a rifled flintlock carbine.

---

[11] Windrow, Martin, *Military dress of North America 1665–1970* (New York, 1973), p.16.
[12] Ibid.
[13] Ibid.

Plate G: Canadian regulars and militia

Figure 1: Soldier, *Compagnies franches de la Marine*, 1690

From their arrival in Canada during the early 1680s, the *Compagnies franches de la Marine* were dressed with a grey-white coat having blue cuffs and lining. Pocket flaps were set low on the hip on each side. Until about 1700, the buttons of the coat were of brass, then of pewter until 1716. Waistcoat, breeches and stockings were grey-white until 1716, when their colour was changed to blue. The *Compagnies franches de la Marine* serving in Acadia and Newfoundland, instead, had blue waistcoat, breeches and stockings from about 1700. The headgear was a black tricorn hat trimmed with 'false gold' and having a black cockade; until

1714, companies in Acadia and Newfoundland had plain hats with no trimming and cockade. In general terms, this uniform was practically identical to that worn by the marines serving on board the French warships: the only difference was that colonial soldiers had coats with no collar, the latter being introduced for the *Compagnies franches de la Marine* only in 1759. The dress worn by colonial regulars in the new territory of Mississipi before 1716 is unknown. They later adopted the same uniform worn by the companies of New France, but with a red waistcoat. Regarding the dress of sergeants, until 1716 they wore distinctive uniforms, having different colours from those of their men. Sergeants serving in New France had grey-white coats with red cuffs, waistcoat, breeches and stockings; those serving in Acadia and Newfoundland had blue coats with red cuffs, waistcoat, breeches and stockings. In both cases the headgear was the usual tricorn hat. In 1716, all sergeants adopted the same colours worn by their men; as rank distinction, they wore gold laced buttonholes on the cuffs. Uniforms for officers became mandatory only in 1732, until which time they were mostly dressed in the same colours as their men, but with additional gold lace on the waistcoats. Officers were not allowed to wear lace on their coats, but were required to have gilded gorgets while on duty. Drummers were dressed in the colours of the royal livery: blue coat with red cuffs and lining. Royal livery lace (a white chain on crimson ground) was later added to the uniforms of drummers, in Acadia and Newfoundland from 1700, and in New France from 1716. In 1716, all drummers serving in America adopted red waistcoat, breeches and stockings.

Since their foundation, the *Compagnies franches de la Marine* were armed with flintlock muskets and swords, having no pikes. The only exception were the companies serving in Newfoundland, which had matchlock muskets until 1700. The flintlock muskets were of the Navy model, being produced in the excellent factory of Tulle in France. These initially had plug bayonets, which were gradually replaced by socket ones (from 1708 in Newfoundland, 1716 in Mississipi and 1721 in New France). Sergeants had halberds and officers had spontoons. While on campaign, polearms and swords were usually replaced by hatchets and knives. The soldier represented in the plate is wearing the practical campaign dress used during winter: for comfort and convenience, the tricorn hat has been replaced by a soft fatigue cap of white-grey cloth, having a blue bottom band and decorative fleur-de-lys. Stockings have been replaced by simpler and more practical Indian-style leggings, which could have various kinds of fringes or other decorations. Shoes have been replaced by moccasins. The hooded Canadian capot was perfect for use during winter; note also the protective cover for the flintlock musket. To move more easily on snow, the soldier is wearing Canadian snowshoes.

Figure 2: Militiaman, Canadian Militia, 1690
During the period under examination, Canadian militiamen had no uniforms and were thus clothed in their own civilian items of dress. Our figure is perfectly dressed and equipped to campaign and survive in the harsh climatic conditions of Canadian winters, with fur hat, dark blue hooded capot, protective gloves, leggings with decorative fringes and moccasins. The firearm that Canadian militiamen preferred using was the solid but light hunting flintlock musket produced at Tulle, having no bayonet. In addition, they were usually armed with hatchets and several knives.

Plate H: Native Americans

Figure 1: Warrior, Wampanoag Confederacy, 1621

Before the arrival of the English settlers, the Wampanoag Indians lived in south-eastern Massachusetts and Rhode Island. They were semi-sedentary and had corn, beans and squash as the staples of their diet, supplemented by what was obtained by fishing and hunting. From a political point of view, the Wampanoags were organized into a confederacy of tribes, which was guided by a head chief. All Wampanoag political leaders were known as 'sachems'. Early relations with the Massachusetts colonists, at the time of Squanto and Massasoit, were generally quite good, but the situation changed dramatically with the progression of the century, mainly as a result of King Philip's political ascendancy. After decades of peace, the Wampanoags showed all their military potential and great skills as bush fighters. The New England colonists, despite having superior weapons, were defeated by them on several occasions before learning how to counter Indian tactics in an effective way. Following King Philip's death and their final defeat in the war, only 400 Wampanoags survived. Here we have represented an early Wampanoag warrior, dating back to the time of Massasoit: the first Indians met by the Pilgrim Fathers must have looked very similar to this figure. No European weapons or pieces of equipment are carried. The young warrior is still armed with the traditional arms of his tribe, which included bows, knives and wooden war clubs. Note the use of a sea turtle shell as a bag, typical of the Indian tribes living on the Atlantic.

Figure 2: Warrior, Huron Nation, 1649

From the arrival of the French in Canada, the Hurons were among their most important and loyal allies. The long hostility between them and the Iroquois already existed, but the military alliance with the French and the contrasting interests over control of the fur trade were the main causes that led to open war between the two tribes. Being more numerous and better armed with modern European muskets, the Iroquois occupied Huronia and killed most of its inhabitants. After these terrible events, however, the Hurons continued to exist and remained loyal allies of the French until the fall of New France. Unlike what many people may suppose, Indian warriors of the seventeenth and eighteenth centuries were frequently equipped with protective armour and shields. This was the case with the Iroquois and, on a larger scale, the Hurons. Indian armour was quite simple, being made of pieces of wood laced together with cords, mainly intended as a protection against enemy arrows. Wooden greaves were also in use, as well as shields of different sizes and shapes (but always made of wood). With the progress of time, the Indian warriors soon learned that their armour and shields were of no practical use against the modern weapons employed by the Europeans. As a result, their use gradually declined during the first decades of the eighteenth century. Armour very similar to that shown here, albeit made with different materials, was used by the native inhabitants of Alaska and Siberia until the twentieth century. The offensive weapons of our warrior are a bow and a wooden war club: the latter could have many different shapes and decorations, usually resembling wild animals or other elements related to the traditional religion of the natives.

Bibliography

Primary sources

Adams, James Truslow, *The Founding of New England* (Boston, 1921)

Andrews, Charles M., *Colonial Self-Government, 1652–1689* (New York, 1904)

Andrews, Charles M., *The Colonial Period of American History* (New Haven, 1934–1938)

Crane, Verner W., *The Southern Frontier, 1670–1732* (Durham, 1928)

Greene, Evarts Boutelle, *Provincial America, 1690–1740* (New York, 1905)

Weeden, William Babcock, *Economic and Social History of New England, 1620–1789* (Boston, 1890)

Secondary sources

Asquith, Stuart, *New Model Army 1645–1660* (London, 1981)

Barthorp, Michael, *Marlborough's Army 1702–1711* (London, 1980)

Blaxland, Gregory, *The Buffs* (London, 1972)

Brzezinski, Richard, *The Army of Gustavus Adolphus Volume 1 (Infantry)* (London, 1991)

Brzezinski, Richard, *The Army of Gustavus Adolphus Volume 2 (Cavalry)* (London, 1993)

Carman, W.Y., *The Royal Artillery* (London, 1973)

Chartrand, René, *The French Soldier in Colonial America* (Ottawa, 1984)

Chartrand, René, *Louis XIV's Army* (London, 1988)

Chartrand, René, *Canadian Military Heritage (Volume 1, 1000–1754)* (Montreal, 1993)

Chartrand, René, *Colonial American Troops 1610–1774 (1)* (Oxford, 2002)

Chartrand, René, *Colonial American Troops 1610–1774 (2)* (Oxford, 2002)

Chartrand, René, *Colonial American Troops 1610–1774 (3)* (Oxford, 2003)

Chartrand, René, *French Fortresses in North America 1535–1763* (Oxford, 2005)

Chartrand, René, *The Forts of New France (1)* (Oxford, 2008)

Chartrand, René, *The Forts of New France (2)* (Oxford, 2010)

Chartrand, René, *The Forts of Colonial North America* (Oxford, 2011)

Chartrand, René, *French Musketeer 1622–1775* (Oxford, 2013)

Childs, John, *Warfare in the Seventeenth Century* (London, 2001)

Fraser, David, *The Grenadier Guards* (London, 1989)

Gallay, Allan, *Colonial Wars of North America 1512–1763: An Encyclopedia* (New York & London, 1996)

Grant, Charles S., *From Pike to Shot 1685–1720* (London, 1986)

Haythornthwaite, Philip J., *The English Civil War, 1642–1651: An Illustrated Military History* (London, 1998)

Heath, Ian, *The Armies of England, Scotland, Ireland, the United Provinces and the Spanish Netherlands 1487–1609* (Guernsey, 1997)

Heath, Ian, *The Armies of the Aztec and Inca Empires, Other Native Peoples of the Americas, and the Conquistadores 1450–1608* (Guernsey, 1999)

Johnson, Michael G., *American Woodland Indians* (London, 1990)

Johnson, Michael G., *American Indians of the Southeast* (London, 1995)

Johnson, Michael G., *Tribes of the Iroquois Confederacy* (Oxford, 2003)

Johnson, Michael G., *Indian Tribes of the New England Frontier* (Oxford, 2006)

Johnson, Michael G., *North American Indian Tribes of the Great Lakes* (Oxford, 2011)

Konstam, Angus, *Pirates 1660–1730* (Oxford, 1998)

Konstam, Angus, *Buccaneers 1620–1700* (Oxford, 2000)

Konstam, Angus, *Pirate: the Golden Age* (Oxford, 2011)

Konstam, Angus, *Warships of the Anglo-Dutch Wars 1652–1674* (Oxford, 2011)

Leach, Douglas Edward, *Arms for Empire: a Military History of the British Colonies in North America 1607–1763* (New York, 1973)

Lustig, Mary, *The Imperial Executive in America, Sir Edmund Andros, 1637–1714* (Cranbury, 2002)

Nellis, Eric, *An Empire of Regions: A Brief History of Colonial British America* (Toronto, 2010)

Peterson, Harold L., *Arms and Armor in Colonial America* (New York, 1956)

Pieroni, Piero, *I grandi capi Indiani* (Florence, 1964)

Roberts, Keith, *Soldiers of the English Civil War Volume 1 (Infantry)* (London, 1989)

Roberts, Keith, *Soldiers of the English Civil War Volume 2 (Cavalry)* (London, 1990)

Roberts, Keith, 'The Virginia Militia', in *Military Illustrated* No.61, June/July 1993

Roberts, Keith, *Matchlock Musketeer* (Oxford, 2002)

Tincey, John, *The British Army 1660–1704* (London, 1994)

Tincey, John, *Ironsides* (Oxford, 2002)

Tisdale, D.A., *Soldiers of the Virginia Colony, 1607–1699* (Petersburg, 2000)

Ward, Harry M., *The United Colonies of New England 1643–1690* (New York, 1961)

Webb, Stephen, *1676: The End of American Independence* (Syracuse, 1995)

Windrow, Martin, *Military Dress of North America 1660–1970* (New York, 1973)

Young, Peter, *The English Civil War Armies* (London, 1994)

Zaboly, Gary, *American Colonial Ranger* (Oxford, 2004)

Index